Surgeon Unmasked

Surgeon Unmasked

A JOURNEY FROM SHAME TO GRACE

DAVID HOCKMAN, MD

SURGEON UNMASKED
A Journey from Shame to Grace

Cover Design by Abigael Elliot
Interior Layout and Design by Alice Briggs
Editorial Team: Jeffery Miller, Ginny Glass, Marcie Taylor, Rachel Maier

ISBN E-book: 979-8-89165-729-8
ISBN Paperback: 979-8-89165-730-4
ISBN Hardcover: 979-8-89165-731-1

Published by:
Streamline Books
Kansas City, MO
shareyourstory.com

For Sherry, my wife, my life, my home

To the following readers: the ones who aspire to make their life's work a ministry, anyone who has suffered from spiritual abuse and considered giving up on God, those who have suffered from or are in a relationship with someone who suffers from chronic physical or mental illness, and the young adults who aspire to a career in medicine and surgery.

I hope my story of serving others and glorifying God by helping people walk will inspire you to love and serve God with your whole heart and to love your neighbor as yourself.

I hope my journey out of spiritual abuse and into a deep, abiding, loving, secure relationship with God will inspire you to place your hope and faith in God and never in man.

I hope my battle with depression and anxiety during my successful career will inspire you to be kind to others who may be suffering with mental illness, to persevere through your own trials with self-compassion, to never give up hope, to avoid self-medication through addictive behavior, and finally to trust our good and sovereign God, knowing that "He who began a good work in you will bring it to completion at the day of Jesus Christ" (Philippians 1:6).

Soli Deo gloria!

CONTENTS

PROLOGUE

A CHILD IS HOME alone. His parents are working at their hardware store two blocks down the road. The boy is looking for a lost toy and screams, "Sh*t! Where is that d*mn thing?"

His next thought is surprising, even to him. "What if they have recorders around the house to catch me if I cuss?"

The poor soul begins looking around the house for recording devices. Finally, he convinces himself that there are likely none but that he'll only know for sure after his parents return home. If he gets caught, then he overlooked a hidden recorder. If he goes to bed without any trouble, then he's OK.

"But what if they wait to listen until after I go to sleep?"

Knowing he'll likely have to go to bed wondering, he heads to the bathroom to begin his bedtime routine. He washes his hands, brushes his teeth, heads to his bedroom, walks past the water heater, and climbs onto his captain's bed across from the workbench, which is now his dresser. Technically, he is sleeping in a utility room, which was converted into his bedroom to put some distance between him and his brother and their constant fighting. The washer and dryer had been moved out of the utility room and into the kitchen to make way for his bed.

Stretching out and relaxing would feel so good. He's tempted to do it, but he fears an intruder may tickle him in his sleep, so he keeps his arms down by his side. If they drift up while he is awake, he quickly draws them back down. It's so hard to get to sleep, knowing he may get in trouble in the morning for cussing and hoping no one tickles him. His mind races until sleep finally brings relief.

The next morning, all is clear. It was a close call, but he's not in trouble. He arises early for the one-hour drive to church on Sunday morning. His best clothes are the only ones that God wants to see in His house of worship. So he puts on his only pair of slacks, a button-down shirt, and shiny shoes. The family drives past scores of other churches to get to the "one true church," the "sound" church on Kingsmere Lane in Kansas City.

It's Christmas Sunday. The class before worship service (which is *not* called "Sunday school" because that would be unscriptural) avoids discussing Jesus's birth, the acapella hymns are not carols but dirges, and the sermon is entitled, "Why We Don't Celebrate Christmas."

When the service is over, the good times begin when all the kids go outside and roll down the hill and play King of the Mountain. The games end about as quickly as they start because the boy knows he must return that evening if he wants to be right with God. That's four hour-long car rides in a single day. And there will be two more on Wednesday night.

In all, six hours of driving and three hours of church are mandatory each week if you want to have your name in the Lamb's Book of Life. This boy is not even sure if his name is in that book. As best he knows, based on what he's been taught, God erases names more often than He writes them down. One thing he is sure of (or at least, he's been told it's sure) is that the names of people in other churches are definitely not in the book.

This knowledge hasn't helped him make friends in school. He thinks, *If God only* maybe *accepts me, and for sure does not accept kids who go to other churches, then why would these kids ever consider accepting me? They all seem to know each other because they see each other on Sundays in local churches. I'm the weird one.*

The boy grows up filled with shame, trusting only one thing. He will be a successful and wealthy doctor because he is smart. The one thing he holds on to through all the storms of childhood is his intelligence. He will prove to all those "lost" kids that he has worth, that he is not a freak. Oh, and there's one other thing that is guaranteed: He will never, ever leave the "one true church."

"What shall a man profit if he gains the whole world and loses his own soul?" So sayeth the Scriptures. The boy knows without a doubt that he will toe the company line throughout eternity. He will "not grow weary in doing good." Though a successful doctor, he will remain convicted of his Conservative Church of Christ doctrine because otherwise, he will face the fires of hell.

Or so he thinks.

Hello, my name is David, and I am a recovering child of the Conservative Churches of Christ. It has been twenty years since I've been inside a Church of Christ building, but its influence on my life still haunts me.

Welcome to my story.

INTRODUCTION

IN THEIR ZEAL to evangelize, some churches go door-to-door, knocking and hoping for an opening. The twenty-something Mormons show up in pairs, wearing white shirts, black ties, and "Elder" name tags. Jehovah's Witnesses knock on the doors while holding *Watchtower* magazines. Some evangelicals hand out invitations to tent revivals at every home in a neighborhood. But Conservative Church of Christ (CCOC) preachers are a bit more stealthy. They prefer to pop up out of nowhere in a person's life and offer a better way. Whether at home, at work, or at play, CCOC people are always anxious to invite people to "Bible studies," which is their covert way of proselytizing.

And so, in 1967, Andrew A. Wandrin showed up for a pecan log roll and a tank of gas at the local Stuckey's store—"a roadside oasis [of] souvenirs, cold drinks, hot snacks, and pecan candy." As a devout CCOC preacher, he was always looking for a listening ear, and he found two pairs in Glendy and Eva Hockman. Having left their home state of Kentucky, Glendy and Eva had just moved to Michigan to manage the local Stuckey's store. With no friends and no family, they were ripe for the picking when Andrew invited the young couple to a Bible study. Glendy and Eva had been looking for an Independent Christian Church, but the only nearby churches were Catholic, Lutheran, and CCOC. Andrew offered to show them the way of the Scriptures more accurately, which, in his mind, led straight to the CCOC.

Glendy was no stranger to God's word. He grew up attending an Independent Christian Church in his hometown in Kentucky. His father was a jovial elder there, and his mother had a reputation as the sweetest, but orneriest, woman you'd ever want to know. Glendy was baptized at that Christian church, and his younger brother Ray was ordained as a minister there. Even Glendy's youngest brother, Kyle, was a deacon there later in life. It's safe to say Glendy was entrenched right in the middle of the Restoration Movement.

Allow me to digress a moment. The Restoration Movement, also known as the Stone-Campbell Movement, began in the early nineteenth century by former Presbyterian Barton W. Stone and by former Presbyterians Thomas and Alexander Campbell, who became Baptists. Disillusioned by denominational divisions and creeds, they sought to unite Christians by returning to the simplicity of the first-century apostolic church described in the New Testament. Followers of the movement, often referred to as Campbellites, believed that human creeds and traditions cause division and that following New Testament examples, such as believers' baptism by immersion and weekly communion, was the key to Christian unity.

Ultimately, internal tensions over issues like missionary societies and instrumental music in worship led to divisions. The splintered movement now includes (from right wing to left wing) Conservative Churches of Christ, mainstream Churches of Christ, the Independent Christian Church, and Disciples of Christ.

Back to my dad. Why he would entertain the demands of the extreme right wing of that movement is a mystery, especially when he had become accustomed to a Baptist church while serving in the Air Force.

Eva, on the other hand, did not grow up in a strongly Christian home. Her father was an alcoholic who refused to attend the Methodist church with his family. Thus, Eva grew up knowing about Jesus, but it wasn't until she met Glendy that she began taking her faith seriously.

She was fifteen when she met Glendy, four years her senior, and eighteen when she married him. Their first few years of marriage were happy ones, but like most couples, they were filled with financial challenges and family drama. Moving to Michigan provided better-paying jobs to the young couple as well as a possible escape.

Perhaps feeling lonely and isolated, Glendy and Eva listened intently to the cultish ramblings of Andrew Wandrin. The idea of a perfected Christian orthodoxy and orthopraxy appealed to them as they sought truth and community. Eventually, under Andrew's influence, they were rebaptized and became proponents of what they felt was the "one true church."

The journey started so innocently. Hundreds of miles from home, this young couple needed a support network, and Andrew Wandrin, his wife, and the CCOC provided instant friendship within a tight-knit community. When their firstborn son, Dan, arrived in the summer of 1968, the employees at Stuckey's and their families in the CCOC were eager to pitch in and serve as an extended family. Ultimately, it would be the same with the CCOC every time the Hockmans moved because one of the primary tenants of the CCOC's unwritten rules is to avoid outsiders and cling to one another—a perfect recipe for a lonely, shame-ridden childhood. And that is what I had.

Chapter 1

Early Influences and Indoctrination

In a Sea of Emptiness

In a sea of emptiness
I am drowning
Searching for you.

In darkness,
I groan,
Hopelessly looking for you.

Though the sun, moon, and stars
Fell on the day
We lost you,

If you returned
We would glow
In your radiant presence.

I GREW UP IN my family's hardware store. Every day after school, I'd walk to the store and then to Branum Rexall Drugs to get a soda and a candy bar. Then my older brother Dan and I would head to the store's back room and watch cartoons. After snack time, we might play in the alleyway behind the store. If business was slow, we'd fool around with the merchandise, making toy guns with pipe fittings. Sometimes, we'd get the extension ladder out, climb up on the roof, and watch the traffic go by or dare each other to walk along the edge. Other times, we'd go upstairs to the mysterious second floor, which used to be an old dance hall. Dancing was a big no-no in the CCOC, so playing up there felt as risky as walking on the edge of the building's roof. Whatever we decided to do, we felt free.

We also learned to work. Dad taught us to assemble lawn mowers and bicycles before we were ten years old. By twelve, we were fixing broken windows, helping customers find the items they needed, and ringing them up on the cash register. We loved it.

I was born in June 1971 in Oak Grove, Missouri, one year after Glendy and Eva had moved from Michigan to Missouri to own their own business, which was called DX (similar to Stuckey's). A year later, tired of working the same Stuckey's schedule of seven days per week, they sold the DX and purchased a hardware store on the corner of Broadway and Twelfth Street, and that became the setting for my childhood. From then on, they worked Monday to Saturday, ten hours a day, and Dan and I were with them much of that time.

On Sundays, we had church obligations. Unfortunately, the Church of Christ in Oak Grove was not conservative enough for them, so we began taking thrice-weekly trips to another town to find what Mom and Dad considered a "sound" church. In the CCOC, the definition of a "sound" church was unwritten but understood to include things like opposition to using the church building for eating meals together and opposition to using the church's money for supporting orphans' homes, church publications, missionary societies, or Bible colleges.

At first, they chose a twenty-minute drive to King City, but after a few years, that church proved unsound in teaching that you will not lose your salvation for one sin. Consequently, we left and drove forty-five minutes to Kansas City, a routine we kept up for about five years. Eventually, they left the KC church to begin a new church about ten miles from home with three or four other families. With a mere fifteen-minute drive, it felt like a small victory. However, four years later, that church decided to join forces with the "unsound" King City church, and we left once again. Finally, they settled on a thirty-five-minute drive east of Kansas City, where we would remain for twenty years.

In fact, I never attended a church in my hometown. And those long drives happened multiple times per week. We went on Sunday mornings for Bible study and worship, then Sunday evenings for more worship, and finally Wednesday evenings for more Bible study. The road trips were a sacrifice my parents were willing to make because they sincerely believed in and loved Jesus, and they wanted more than anything for their boys to feel the same way. But, as a kid, I wasn't a fan of being stuck in the car for so long.

The CCOC was opposed to a legion of things, but one thing they supported wholeheartedly was attendance. Oh, and you couldn't just show up. In the '70s and '80s, you had to dress up for God while also keeping your kids quiet and looking happy to be there. It felt like you either earned God's favor by showing up correctly or risked His wrath by missing. In the CCOC, every sin you commit forces God to scratch your name out of the Lamb's Book of Life, including missing church. If you follow the forgiveness formula of repenting and praying, He writes your name back in. God's words in Scripture were always used to back up every belief. So suffice it to say, we never missed unless we were sick, real sick. This always confused me. I could never figure out why we had to try so hard to please God if He loved us as much as the rest of Scripture said He did.

Now, my earliest memories of going to church were not entirely unpleasant. After all, going to church meant being together as a family. Though the car rides seemed long, we would sometimes stop for ice cream on the way home, which made the trip feel worthwhile. At the Kansas City church, my children's class teacher was tall, thin, and pretty. I was sure I'd marry her someday. The other kids were fun and inclusive. While our parents were busy socializing after services, we'd play King of the Hill or roll down the hill until we were dizzy and covered in grass stains. We had a good time once our church duty was over.

I was devastated when I was told we had to leave that Kansas City church of two hundred people to start a small, new church with no other boys my age. I was in third grade, and my beautiful teacher had told me, if I memorized Psalm 23 and recited it perfectly, she would give me my own Bible with my name embossed on the cover. I had Psalm 23 ready to regurgitate. I didn't understand all of it, but I could repeat it word-for-word. Thankfully, I convinced my mom and dad to go one more Sunday, all the way to Kansas City. I saw my Sunday school crush one last time and returned home with a new, red leather-bound King James Bible, with "David" written in gold letters in the lower right-hand corner. I still have this prized possession as a reminder to me of one of the greatest benefits I received while in the CCOC—a wide breadth of biblical knowledge.

It would have been nice to brag about my accomplishment the next day and show off my new Bible, but I didn't have any good friends in Oak Grove to show and tell. From the first day of kindergarten, it was apparent to me that most of the kids in town already knew each other either from going to church together or from their parents growing up in town. No one seemed too interested in making new friends, as they already had defined friend groups. Grant, Marcus, Julie, and many others knew each other from the Baptist church. James, Violet, and a few others went to the Methodist church. Violet told me once that she loved being a Methodist because "You can smoke or drink, and it's OK with God." I didn't have the heart to tell her (or any of them) that I was taught they were all going to hell. At the time, my parents only socialized with members of their church, so I had little opportunity to make friends with classmates outside of school.

The first friends I made outside of church were my neighbors across the street. I grew up two blocks away from Hockman Hardware in a small two-bedroom, one-bathroom Victorian home on Broadway. Parker and Brent Delton lived across the street. Parker and my brother were a year apart, as were Brent and I. We built forts together, played Cops and Robbers, rode bikes, and even occasionally fought each other.

Although the Rogers family did not go to church, my mom let us play together, not knowing that they would teach my brother and me how to cuss like sailors. We even discovered pornography in a Ziplock bag one day during a bike ride when I was eight or nine years old. I didn't know what I was looking at, but just as I was drawn to my Sunday school teacher's "covered beauty," I was enthralled at the uncovered female form. When we went back to the secret spot days later, the treasure was gone. To my delight and later shame, I would occasionally get to see more pornography at my cousins' house on our family's semiannual trips to Kentucky.

Parker and Brent eventually moved across town when I was about ten years old, which ended our friendship since we never saw them in the classrooms. Making friends was constantly a battle. I felt ashamed that my family thought everyone else was going to hell for not being in the "one true church." My big brown eyes, crooked teeth, bowl haircut, and lack of confidence made me self-conscious. Trying to fit in didn't work when you had to be perfect and couldn't trust anyone. Yet, the kids at school seemed so at ease with themselves and each other. At home, on Sunday nights, I could stand on the top of the couch and sing at the top of my lungs, "Well, we're movin' on up," with the Jeffersons on TV, but the next day at school, I was quiet and invisible.

My parents had no idea that there were two Davids. The confident one stayed at home. The insecure one went to school and struggled to find connection. During first grade, the insecure David was absent more than thirty days due to illnesses ranging from measles to pneumonia. I visited the doctor's office almost as much as I visited the church building.

The secure David felt better after every visit and wanted to be just like his doctor one day. I saw the doctor's new Porsche in the parking lot and reasoned that doctors must have it made. Every February, business in the hardware store would slow down, and I complained about eating ground beef at every meal. My parents would reprimand me by saying, "It's better than eating beans like we used to." I hated beans, so fair enough. February taught me that we were just getting by, and I knew that, by becoming a doctor, I could not only help people feel better but also do more than simply get by. With a head full of dreams, I'd return to school after each illness, struggle to catch up, and return to being the insecure David.

In third grade, a new kid moved to town, and I decided to be brave and try to make a friend. Hank was a bit of a trouble-maker, but I was no angel either. One Friday at recess, I shared a dirty little rhyme I made up. I still remember it: "E B Doh, E B Dah, Stick a motherf*cker in your bra." He looked me straight in the eye with no hesitation and said, "I'm telling on you! I'm telling unless you give me a piece of gum from your dad's hardware store."

What an evil little brat! I couldn't believe it. His first response to my attempt at friendship was to blackmail me! No wonder I didn't trust anyone. I went to Hockman Hardware after school that day and got some pennies out of the cash register. Like always, I bought myself some gum, but unlike always, I also got some for Hank. In fear, I kept silent all weekend as we made our multiple trips to church in Kansas City. Secrecy and hiding behind a mask of happiness begin early in the CCOC.

Even if I'd told my parents about Hank's blackmail, I wasn't sure they would be of much help. In my limited experience, protecting our family name was of paramount importance. The Bible commands us to abstain from every form of evil (1 Thessalonians 5:22). Jesus may have hung out with the prostitutes and sinners, but we couldn't risk our good name. Though the Bible is filled with verses about trusting God and having no fear, the message I received was just the opposite. We had to maintain a good reputation to keep a livable income at the hardware store. Although certainly unintentional, the notion to "trust self more than God" was a constant theme.

Having my jean jacket stolen exemplifies this quite well. I was in first grade and had the coolest jean jacket you could imagine. It was covered in patches from the local auto parts store, from my dad's hardware store, and from the Kentucky police department, where my uncle worked. One day, it was stolen and claimed by Dicky Packer. Distraught, I told my mom and dad as soon as I got home to the hardware store.

When Mom went to talk to my teacher, she discovered that my name wasn't on the jacket. That was it. She said I had to let it go since I couldn't prove it was mine, never mind that it was my prized possession or that it had a unique Kentucky PD patch. Never mind the fact that no other kid would have access to our hardware store's patches. No, she and Dad let the school have their way, and I lost the jacket permanently. Looking back, I think they just wanted to avoid conflict. Or perhaps it was their interpretation of Luke 6:29: "To the one who strikes you on the cheek, offer the other also, and from one who takes away your cloak do not withhold your tunic either." Maybe they speculated that Dickey needed it more than I. At the time, I didn't know and didn't care. I just wanted my beloved jacket back.

Ultimately, it didn't matter why they didn't fight for me. What I learned from that experience was that I needed to take care of myself. The next day, I snuck to the back of the class and wrote my name in the jacket with a permanent black ink pen. I got caught in the act, and no one came to my defense.

The lesson of the stolen jacket was likely in the back of my mind when Hank was blackmailing me, so on Monday morning, I approached him with stolen gumballs in hand and said, "Here you go, Hank. Now leave me alone."

He ripped the gum out of my hand and said, "I want gum tomorrow, too!" Fear of parents, fear of teachers, and fear of punishment gripped my eight-year-old heart, and I said, "Fine." I walked away and told no one. I was too ashamed, too afraid— typical feelings for a CCOC boy.

After school, I went to the store, grabbed some pennies, and got more gum: some for me and some for Hank. The next day, I said, "Here's your gum. Now come on, Hank, leave me alone."

But he said, "I've seen those Mean Joe Green and Terry Bradshaw Pittsburgh Steelers cards you have. I want 'em, or I'm telling."

"No way," I cried.

He again threatened to tell, so in fear, I resigned, "Fine."

Alone, isolated, and fearful—what a state for a third grader. I just couldn't let my parents find out that I had said the *F* word. I would disappoint them, and they might condemn me to ten swats with a belt on the bare behind. That was the punishment I received for the big transgressions. I feared Dad's ten swats as much as my name being blotted out of the Lamb's Book of Life. Thankfully, those spankings were rare, as Mom was the principal disciplinarian.

One time, I got spanked so hard that my dad asked to see my bare butt the next morning to make sure he didn't leave a mark. My brother and I had been sent upstairs at the hardware store to remove the water that had collected from our perpetually leaking roof. Despite our annual Thanksgiving and Easter tarring of the roof cracks, it still leaked. What we really needed was a new roof, but we couldn't afford it. Instead, Dad used to put kiddie pools under the leaky areas.

Well, that day, he sent us upstairs to use a sump pump to remove the water from the pools, draining it through a hose stuck out the window. But Dan had a better idea. "Let's just pick up the pool and pour it out the window."

"No, Dad said use the pump and hose," I said.

"This will be faster," he insisted. "Come on, let's get this done and go play."

I had no choice. He was bigger than me. So we picked up one end of the kiddie pool and promptly dumped the whole thing on the floor. Water gushed out across the room, then seeped through the floor and poured onto the merchandise below.

Furious, my father scolded us about damaging the business that put food on our table. That was fair, but the fierce spanking when we got home was not.

I never wanted to experience a spanking like that again, so when Hank demanded my prized Steelers cards, I felt I had no choice. When I got home that day, I took out the Mean Joe Green and Terry Bradshaw cards for one last look at the stats and pictures. Then I tucked them between the pages of my schoolbooks.

The next morning, Wednesday, I gave the cards to Hank. He took them and immediately demanded a dollar. Where was God? Where was my dignity? I couldn't find either. In fear, I went home and stole a dollar from the cash register. I stole to hide my sin. I stole because I was being sinned against. Sin was leaving permanent marks on my life, and fear was isolating me. That pattern would recur throughout my childhood. Nevertheless, I kept my little happy CCOC mask on tightly and dutifully went to Wednesday night church in Kansas City.

Thursday, I proclaimed, "Here's your dollar, Hank. I'm done!"

But Hank responded, "No, you aren't. You're doing it again tomorrow."

I finally reached a breaking point. I was fed up. I should have been fed up sooner, I know, but fear makes you behave irrationally. Anyway, I broke my silence and told my only buddy, Clay. He couldn't believe I was so easily manipulated. Clay had the perfect solution: denial.

That had never occurred to me. As Clay explained, "Mrs. Lore [our homeroom teacher] loves us! She is never going to believe that you would say something like that. Plus, she doesn't like Hank at all. There's no way she'll believe him!"

Clay's plan seemed solid, but I was still scared. Lying would just add to my long list of sins. I went home with my happy mask firmly in place, but I was riddled with fear. What if the plan didn't work? Damnation with ten swats on the bare butt with a belt—that's what.

Thank God the next day was Friday! As before, Hank approached me and said, "Where's my dollar?"

Feigning confidence, I replied, "Forget it, Hank! No more. Tell on me, if you want. I don't care! I'll just deny it, and Mrs. Lore will never believe you!"

"Fine," Hank mumbled. And that was it! The ordeal was over. After all that torture, he dropped it, just like that. I couldn't believe it. All that fear had been for nothing. After I related this story while preaching at a men's conference, I thought it best to tell my parents about it first. They were deeply saddened by my fear and shame and wished I had come to them for help. That just didn't seem possible at the time, but I was thankful for their gracious response.

Unfortunately, while the blackmailing stopped, the bullying did not. Whether from kids at school, the teaching at church, or my own negative self-talk, I felt like I was constantly under attack.

I think my friendship with Clay provides a perfect example of the way the CCOC's judgmental teaching had worked its way into our home. You see, Clay's parents were divorced, and he lived with his mother and her boyfriend of many years. When Clay invited me for a sleepover, my parents said, "Absolutely not." Although his mother and boyfriend were kind and caring people, my parents believed they were unfit to care for me overnight because of their scandalous lifestyle. When I had to break the news to Clay that I couldn't spend the night at his house, I felt ashamed.

Clay didn't seem to mind my family's attitude. For a kid growing up in a "sinful home," he sure was loving and accepting, yet I could never fully trust that he liked me. After all, I never felt good enough to be loved and accepted by a demanding Supreme Being, so how could I ever be good enough for one of His lesser created beings? Once, when Clay's mother's boyfriend was out of town, I got to spend the night with him. We had a great time, though I could not understand the logic behind my parents' decision.

My low self-esteem made me desperate to fit in. Clay liked country music, so I did too. Honestly, I preferred rock 'n' roll. When Clay eventually found out, he said, "David, just because I like country music doesn't mean you have to like it to be my friend."

Grace from Sinners

Oddly enough, I caught my first glimpse of freedom and grace from someone who was trapped in a "sinful home."

As I said, I didn't have many friends, and I wasn't sure what I needed to do to make them. Believing that my classmates were unjustly bound for hell, losing every race at recess, and being picked last for every team sport did not provide a great foundation of confidence. I struggled with how I was to view my classmates. Was I to believe that I was spiritually superior to them simply because I'd been born into a family that took me to the perfect church? That never made sense to me.

Around that time, I began piano lessons, hoping to discover a talent that matched my passion for music. My mammaw played piano by ear, and I loved making a racket on her old upright piano during semiannual trips to Kentucky. However, as it turns out, taking piano lessons was not what cool kids did, and furthermore, I wasn't very good. Rather than endearing me to anyone looking to find friendship through common musical interests, I found that I had made myself a target for increased ridicule.

One day, on the way home from piano lessons, Dicky Packer saw me riding my bike while holding piano books.

"What do you have in your hands, Hockman?" he asked.

I knew this wasn't going to end well, as Dicky was a pretty rough kid and a damn thief. "Nothing," I sheepishly replied.

"Looks like you're a little f*ggot, taking piano lessons!" he screamed as he ran at me.

I had no time to respond, but I don't think I would have even if I did. My parents told me not to fight lest I give our family a bad name. Before I knew it, Dicky tackled me off my bike and had me on the ground, punching me. Somehow, I managed to get away, or maybe he let me go. Either way, I was only ten years old and terrified.

I was close to the school where my brother was practicing football, so I screamed for Dan to help as I rode my bike toward the football field. Pedaling as fast as I could, I crashed my bike and took a tumble. Fearfully, I turned around to see if Dicky was closing in. Thankfully, he was gone. Humiliated at not sticking up for myself and for running away, I slowly made my way home, too ashamed to tell anyone what had happened.

Sin and Fit In

Transitioning to middle school brought a change in environment that I hoped would help me find a friend group. Despite developing a pot belly, which I tried to flatten by doing aerobics with my mom and Jane Fonda, I was becoming more athletic. As it turns out, being athletic is a key factor in being "good enough" to make friends. Suddenly, I started getting picked fourth or fifth for teams instead of last.

Sadly, rather than consoling the new "last kid picked," I belittled him to gain favor with the first. We'd sit at the lunch table and make fun of "those" people. I was finally fitting in, finally finding friends, but in my heart, I knew I was sinning and disappointing God and myself.

One poor soul I tormented was a hemophiliac. He had developed a sarcastic, arrogant way of dealing with his disorder because he knew no one would physically abuse a bleeder. So we verbally abused him. I was torn between feeling sorry for him and feeling more sorry for myself if I didn't join in and make fun of him. He died from AIDS in his thirties. When I read that in the newspaper, I was flooded with remorse for how I'd treated him.

Verbally, I was ruthless, and I knew God must hate me. Still, it was nice to feel like I belonged finally. Guilt and shame riddled the new friendships I was making. How could I trust these people who demanded such horrible behavior as the price of inclusion? How could I trust a god who had nothing better in store for me than to either "sin and fit in" or to obey imperfectly and be condemned?

Chapter 2

AN ELUSIVE ATTEMPT AT SALVATION

Can You See Him

Can you see Him hanging on the tree?
Cursed Son of God for you and me,
High upon Golgotha's lonely hill,
Our sins led Him, the law to fulfill.

Crowned with thorns, enrobed with saving blood,
Equality with God, a thing not robbed,
Despised, rejected, reviled by men,
Death seemed to be the victor again.

Truly this is God's only Son,
Sent from heaven to earth, death to o'ercome.
Nailed to a cross, yet was glorified.
Redeeming mankind, our Savior died.

Holy God, be merciful to me.
I see Your Son, hanging on the tree.

IWAS TWELVE YEARS old when I first realized I might be caught in a trap, gambling with my eternal life. The Churches of Christ teach—much like Jewish tradition—that a child reaches the "age of accountability" at thirteen, so maybe I had a little more time, or perhaps the Church of Christ had gotten the age of accountability wrong. If they were right, then very soon my only shot at salvation would be at baptism—until my next cuss word, at least. And if I forgot to pray about cussing and died in a car wreck? Well, I'd go straight to hell, because the last thing I'd probably say before impact would be, "Oh, sh*t."

As my thirteenth birthday approached, I knew I had a serious decision to make. The CCOC doesn't believe in a sinful nature or original sin. "The soul that sins, it shall die," was their prooftext. So at some point, you're no longer an innocent child destined for eternity with a loving Creator. Apparently, that point was thirteen—when, as if by some mystical shift, you became fully responsible for your sins and damned to hell. At that age, you were believed to know right from wrong, and by your own free will, you chose wrong. No excuses. God's got you dead to rights.

I can see it so clearly. Every CCOC teacher, preacher, or parent would hold up their hand and say that there are five things you must do to be saved and avoid being damned to hell for your sins:

1. (Pointing to the thumb) First, you have to hear.
2. (Pointing to the index finger) Then you must believe.
3. (Pointing to the middle finger) Now, you need to repent of your sins and try hard never to repeat them.

4. (Pointing to the ring finger) Confess that Jesus is the Son of God, who died for our sins and resurrected to give us eternal life.
5. (And finally, pointing to the pinky) Be baptized in water by full immersion in the name of the Father, Son, and Holy Spirit for the remission of sins.

Unfortunately, once you sinned again after your baptism, you were right back to square one—damned to hell.

The CCOC had a formula for that too. If you've sinned and lost your salvation, you pray for forgiveness and repent. But if you keep repeating the same sin, well then, your prayer for forgiveness was likely not sincere. Therefore, to stay secure in your position before God, you essentially need to have no habitual sin.

To my dismay, I already had a habitual sin in my life, which was using swear words. But those four-letter words were so enticing and had such power. How could I give them up? I still struggle with it!

Except for our thrice-weekly trips to church, I managed to bury my head in the sand and ignore the guilt I felt for not doing what I'd been taught was the right thing to do to please God, the church, and my parents. However, each worship service and Bible study turned my stomach in knots. I wasn't ready to take on the responsibility of my own salvation. No one is, but I didn't know that at the time.

One Friday night, the movie *The Day After* was broadcast on television, and it changed everything. We were right in the middle of the Cold War, in a nuclear arms race with Russia, and everyone was afraid of global thermonuclear war. *The Day After* depicted what it might look like, and I couldn't have been more terrified, not even if Dicky Packer was sitting next to me in my own living room. Before the movie ended, I made up some excuse about going to bed early and snuck away to my room. Silent, anxious tears filled my eyes. I knew it was time to lay my cards on the table before God and hope for the best.

I was ready to give my life to Christ, but my dad was suffering from an inguinal hernia and awaiting surgery. Because I wanted my dad to baptize me, procuring my salvation could wait. After all, maybe I was still a child in His eyes. Dad's open hernia repair took months to heal. In the meantime, I worried about my eternal destiny until Dad's strength returned.

I knew I was guilty of my sins. I knew I needed a savior. I trusted God to forgive me because of what Jesus did for me. So finally, one night at church, after Dad had healed up and was feeling well, I told my parents I was ready to be baptized.

Elated, they began filling the baptistry with water right away. We didn't have many baptisms, so the tank usually sat empty. As the ice-cold water poured out, we sang some joyful a cappella hymns until the baptistry was full enough for my total immersion. From what the CCOC had taught me, I knew that as soon as I came up out of that water, my sins would be washed away, and my soul would be as white as snow thanks to the sacrificial blood of Jesus Christ.

I didn't care how cold the water was. I was committed. Still, someone tried to help by setting up an electric space heater nearby and pointing it at the water.

We changed into white baptismal garments, which resembled the garage coveralls some elderly men wear when they give up on fashion and choose comfort and simplicity. Before the baptism, I had reasoned with myself that if the electric heater were left plugged in and fell into the water as I ascended from the baptistry, then it would electrocute me and send me straight to heaven. That seemed like my best chance at staying saved. Not being suicidal, Dad and I ensured the space heater was unplugged before we got in.

The dark red velvet curtains in front of the baptistry opened, revealing my mother's mural of the Jordan River against the back wall. Dad and I walked down the steps into the frigid waters, ready to encounter the healing blood of Jesus Christ.

"David, do you believe that Jesus is God's son and that He died for your sins, was buried, and resurrected to life?" my father asked.

"I do," I affirmed.

"Based on your confession of faith, I now baptize you in the name of the Father, Son, and Holy Spirit," Dad proudly proclaimed as he proceeded to dunk me under the water. As he lifted me up, the curtains closed.

Wanting to make sure Dad got it right, I felt my hair to be sure it was all wet. After all, the CCOC only approved of full immersion baptism. As I patted my head, some of my hair felt dry. I panicked. Dad assured me that I was completely immersed, but I knew if all of me didn't go under, we had not complied with God's will, and God would not save me. I had to get it right.

I didn't trust my dad's answer, so I asked him to dunk me again. During the second immersion, I reached up to my head and rubbed it, as if rinsing out shampoo. It was soaked; I was good, raised from the watery grave to new life. Everyone laughed, thinking we had fallen back in.

Afterward, we drove to McDonald's to celebrate, and for a brief time, I felt my burdens lifted. God had done His part. Now the ball was in my court. All the cussing, gossiping, lusting, and coarse joking had to stop. With all my might and determination, I was set on "being in the world but not of the world."

Chapter 3

BEGINNING THE TRY-HARD/GIVE-UP CYCLE

Lost

Lost in the congregation
Looking for a friend
A connection for confession
A humble transparent Christian

I look in vain
Finding no one
But fearful Christ-followers
Pretending to be unafraid
As they follow their new law

Lost, I need neither the old law
Nor the new for my salvation
My sin is ever before me
The law cannot set me free

My heart cries out for grace
But fear is all I receive
Shame crushes me
As my soul seeks in vain

MY CLASSMATES AND friends noticed the new postbaptismal "me," but they were neither impressed nor supportive. I had told only my one true friend, the Methodist James Garfield, but my group of "friends" noticed the change in my behavior. At the lunch table, the Baptist Marcus Booker asked a typical question about some celebrity: "She's so hot. I'd f*ck her. What about you?"

Silence was my reply. At first, he didn't react, but later, he grew annoyed. "What the f*ck is wrong with you, Hockman? Are you turning gay or something?" he taunted me.

"No, I'm just not going to talk like that," I replied.

"Bullsh*t! You think you're f*cking better than us?" he demanded.

"No," I replied quietly, hoping for a change in conversation.

Little by little, it became clear to everyone in the group that I'd changed.

I didn't flaunt it. I didn't preach or testify. All I did was guard my language a little more closely. Suffering for the sake of Christ was my reward. Pride filled my heart to a small degree. But then the most unusual thing happened. It was as if I had truly become a new person in Christ. I went from sixth grade, going forward to Miss Robinson's desk to ask questions while looking down her blouse at her perfectly tanned breasts, to seventh grade, staying seated, having all the answers, being a straight-A student, and averting my eyes from any lustful opportunity.

Purity in behavior and in grades is a lethal combination for middle school friendships. Gradually, I became increasingly isolated and alone. I knew better than to say anything negative about our church or spiritual lives, so I never discussed these feelings with my family—or anyone, for that matter. My mother had stopped working with my father—something she had done for twenty years—to get a full-time job and obtain health insurance for our family as our coverage had become unaffordable after my father was denied coverage by our then-current provider. She worked nights as a telemarketer, and her absence helped me hide my feelings. I thought, *Why rock the boat? If I just keep quiet, I will keep the peace.*

At the time, I was completely unaware of any labels for my feelings. I knew God expected me to be perfect, so I was a perfectionist, which gave me anxiety. God expected me to "come out from among them" and be separate, so I became lonely, which led to depression. I was a master at hiding my feelings, and the mask I wore at home was impenetrable. At the time, the only diagnosis I had was misery, which was quite the opposite of the promised "peace that surpasses all understanding."

To my family and physician, I was a high-strung overachiever who was ready to take on the world and become a great doctor. To my classmates, I was an awkward straight-A geek. To myself, I was the kid who sometimes sat alone in the bathroom, wondering if I would be better off dead.

Having played the bully in sixth grade, the roles were now reversed. One day, while walking back from shop class, entirely out of the blue, Hank, my former blackmailer, decided to punch me in the kidney. The impact launched my body into the asphalt road between the shop and the middle school. My hands and knees were scraped, and worse, my retainer flew out of my mouth.

Everyone, except a few kind-hearted girls, laughed at me as I searched for my oral appliance and scurried back to class. As was usual, I told no one. Silent, lonely shame became normal for me.

Another day, I caught a glimmer of hope during one of the most isolated times I can remember. Our English teacher wanted us to read aloud to each other. She tried to make it a fun experience by allowing us to go anywhere in the room in pairs or groups. We could sit on a table, under a table, in a corner, anywhere. I had no one to choose, and no one picked me. I'd hit rock bottom, it seemed. I wound up sitting under a table by myself, humiliated and ashamed, with tears streaming down my face. James Garfield saw me, crawled under the table, and started reading to me. No questions asked, just love and grace offered from a Methodist friend.

His kindness was a landmark moment in my life. How could it possibly make sense that a loving God would condemn this Methodist young man with his Christlike heart, who had offered a proverbial "cup of cold water in His name" to a desperate, thirsty member of the "one true church?" How could James be condemned while I was saved? What made me worthier than him? Was it because I was learning to lead singing at church? Maybe having my dad teach me to write and deliver sermons made me more fit for God's kingdom. I wasn't sure, but the whole situation confused me.

CCOC service was all about what you did on Sundays and Wednesdays, but here was a Methodist kid on a Tuesday who showed me more about what it meant to be Jesus than I ever saw in my church. I believe a seed of doubt was planted that day, though it would take decades to grow. One thing was sure: A Methodist loved me unconditionally. He never commented on what happened. He just showed me the grace of Jesus and went on about his day.

Crushed and Humiliated

By eighth grade, God finally gave me the missing ingredient for making small-town friends: a small dose of athleticism. Oak Grove was a classic football town, and playing under the Friday night lights was every boy's dream. I never thought I'd get a chance because I was so slow as a young boy, but I grew athletically in the summer before my last year of junior high.

Earning first-string on both offense and defense for the eighth-grade Panther football team made me suddenly acceptable to my peers. And, quite frankly, beating out Marcus Booker for offensive guard was gratifying given how he had treated me the previous year. Still, I was privately disgusted that my ability on the football field outweighed my classroom performance, my character, and my faith.

The spark of popularity ignited on the gridiron was soon extinguished on the hardwood when I failed to make the basketball team. I loved basketball. When I was little, we had a shed behind our house on Broadway with a basketball goal attached to the eve of the roof. That was the only place I could practice. I had nowhere to dribble the ball except on the narrow, broken sidewalk or the dirt around the goal, where our constant playing had killed off the grass. Even so, I used to dribble and shoot out there for hours.

Later, my father grew tired of our gravel driveway and evidently had a little extra money to pave a blacktop driveway where he installed a basketball goal for us. Now we could play for real. With AC/DC blaring from our little boombox, we played some dangerous hoops in the old neighborhood. The danger was real because our ball often rolled onto the town's main thoroughfare, and we had to dodge traffic to get it back.

When I was twelve, we moved to a three-bedroom house with a concrete driveway in a neighborhood full of teenagers with basketball goals. The only reason we could afford that house was that the foundation had sat empty for five years before someone finally decided to build.

As a lonely seventh grader, I shot hoops at home by myself, but I dreamed of making the team. So when Coach Arshel cut me from the eighth-grade team, I was crushed. Fortunately, largely because of my performance on the football field, I was invited to shoot hoops with my classmate, Dylan Tripp, who lived across the street. We didn't get to play together on the school's team, but thankfully, I had found a friend who was supportive and willing to encourage me that I should have made the team.

I hated Coach Arshel for cutting me. The truth is, he exposed on the outside what I had always felt on the inside—that I was not good enough. Jarod Jones was the last kid to make the cut, and he didn't even show up for the previous few days of tryouts. What's more, he couldn't make a single layup. I knew I was better than him, but Jarod's mom was a teacher across the hall from Coach Arshel. That's how my world worked. I was always on the outside looking in.

Cutting me from the basketball team wasn't the worst thing that Coach Arshel did to me. He also attacked my only sense of self-worth: my grades. Yes, he dared to give me a B in PE one quarter because of my attitude. Granted, my attitude was lousy, so I probably deserved it.

Unfortunately, he also taught (and I mean "taught" in the loosest sense of the word) science, which was my strongest subject. His tests made no sense. Most of us in the class failed the first test, and when that happened, I cried in front of my peers like a widow with a baby on her hip at the graveside service of her dead husband. I mean, I was *inconsolable.* I was humiliated by my own reaction, and Coach Arshel's insensitivity and hatred of children only added to the drama. I eventually got my grade up to an A, but something about that day deeply troubled me. My grades meant too much to me.

Hanging with the Jocks

Scorned by basketball, I decided to wrestle. My elementary school buddy Clay was a wrestler, and I thought it would be fun to try a new sport. I came in third in my first wrestling tournament, but there were only three people in my weight class (including me). Fortunately, I got better and even qualified for the state tournament. I thought wrestling could become my "thing" and give me an identity as a tough guy. Girls liked tough guys, and I finally had my first girlfriend in eighth grade.

By spring, I was also throwing discus in track and had a new friend group: the jocks. My social life was better than ever, yet I often felt lonely, which made no sense to me. Looking back, I think it was depression from the shame that I was feeling.

I was no longer obsessed with repentance, so I soon fell back onto the old path of foul language and lustful thoughts, which took on a whole new dimension as I reached puberty. It's a wonder that I ever discovered masturbation, considering that I had no parental or school education or information about it, but I did. And in doing so, I found an escape from my perfectionism, insecurity, and stress. Thankfully, pornography was difficult to find in my adolescent years, so I didn't get hooked. I knew God's plan only allowed sexual gratification inside marriage, so I tried hard to keep this new sin to a bare minimum (no pun intended).

Transitioning to high school was both exciting and frightening, but I took comfort in my brother's presence as a senior. I knew he would have my back at high school football and wrestling practices. Dan was the MVP of the football team as an offensive right guard and defensive nose guard, atypical positions to be recognized with such a prestigious award.

My brother straddled the fence in his divided senior class, between the "goodies" and the "rowdies." Dan had friends in 4H and student council, as well as friends who are probably doing time in a penitentiary somewhere. I'll never forget seeing two of his rowdy friends on separate occasions knock a kid out with one punch for no reason other than their cruelty. Since Dan had both rough friends and refined friends, I knew no one would mess with me. Still, I felt anxious about this next phase of my life.

My spiritual life had slipped back into old patterns, but the change to high school gave me a good opportunity to shape up. I wasn't as zealous as I had been in seventh grade. I couldn't stand the thought of feeling that isolated again. I wanted to look like a good Christian but not necessarily act like one. I'd tried hard to be perfect, given up, and I was ready to try again, but not so hard this time.

Overall, my freshman year went well. I made straight A's, had close friendships, and was popular with the girls, though my confidence in that department was low. I was well on my way to becoming a doctor. Ultimately, however, my freshman year would mainly serve as a sharp contrast to my sophomore year, which is when I decided to give up again.

Chapter 4

DARK DAYS

My Psalm

Holy God and Father of Mercy
I fear that failure becomes me,

For purity alludes me,
And Your nearness evades me.

My soul is downcast.
My heart is heavy with guilt.

My eyes have wandered.
My thoughts have been unfaithful.

These sins I have dismissed
And counted them for naught.

Denying the truth,
I believed a lie and continued in my sin.

I am burdened.
I am broken.

I am sad.
I am mournful, but I am not alone.

Wretched sinner that I am,
I cast my weary soul at Your feet, begging for purity.

As Job before me, this day I make a covenant with my eyes
Not to look at a woman to lust.

Before You, O Lord, I make this pledge.
I will bring every thought into captivity in obedience to Christ.

In holiness,
I will honor You.

In submission,
I will love You.

In my body and in my spirit,
I will glorify You, Almighty God.

Amen.

AS ONE LAST hurrah before summer's end, my brother and his best friend, Ryan Story, took me and my best friend, James Garfield, to our first rock concert. The band was AC/DC, on their "Who Made Who" World Tour, at Kemper Arena in Kansas City, Sunday, August 3, 1986. During the parking lot party before the concert, Dan offered me an orange Bartles & Jaymes wine cooler, and I liked it. I liked three even better because, for the first time in my short but anxious life, I felt carefree. We rocked out that night, and then the next day, we got in the car with Mom and Dad for our semiannual trip to Kentucky. I was hungover and miserable. Strangely enough, James never partied much after our AC/DC concert together, and unfortunately, we didn't spend much time together after that. I think my soon-to-be extreme behavior pushed him away.

My sophomore year began upon returning from Kentucky, and I found my friendship with my neighbor Dylan growing closer. We had a lot in common. For example, our parents were religious conservatives, and we both grew up with no sisters. He was the youngest of three boys, and I the youngest of two. We just clicked, and I found myself spending more time with him and our mutual older friend, Brad Swindol, a junior, three doors down the road. Brad was also the youngest of two boys, but his parents were divorced. We hung out together all the time, and eventually, we began partying together. I can't recall the first beer we had together, or how we obtained it, or even where we drank it. That whole year runs together like water in a ditch after a downpour. Eventually, I was getting drunk every Friday and Saturday night. How it got to that level escapes me, but I was out of control. I even began to drink on weeknights under the pretense that I was attending a girl's volleyball or basketball game. Initially, I feared I would be unable to maintain my grades, but I somehow managed to do so. At first, I felt guilty about the drinking, but eventually I became defiant. In fact, I felt invincible. It was the most carefree time of my life. I lived for myself, and it finally didn't matter if I was good enough.

Sundays and Wednesdays continued to remind me that I was not. Looking back, I can see that the CCOC doctrine of works-righteousness had killed my desire to be good. If I had to be perfect to be saved, then why try? It was never going to happen anyway. My parents never confided in me that they had struggles too. At the time, in the CCOC, no one ever stepped forward with vulnerable transparency. The preachers and teachers all seemed to have escaped youth without sinful rebellion. Why was I so different? At the time, I felt like a rebel without a cause. I had a stable family. My parents got along well. We went to church. My dad was on the city council. My mom was becoming an independent working woman at a telecommunications company. My brother had a good job and was in college. What did I have to rebel against? We were like the Cunninghams on *Happy Days* or the Cleavers on *Leave It to Beaver*. Just a perfect family except for me, the alcohol abuser, and I was just getting started with my degradation.

As a sophomore, I wrestled in the 132-pound weight class, and it didn't take much to get me buzzed. By the time I was at my peak intake, I was drinking a twelve-pack on Friday and a twelve-pack on Saturday. We used to connect our pull tabs to make a chain. I kept mine in my locker at school, and it was so long that it looped up and down the height of the full-length locker numerous times. I don't know what I was trying to prove, but my favorite song was Pink Floyd's "Comfortably Numb." Also, I could (and still can) recite from memory the Budweiser anthem: "This is the famous Budweiser beer. We know of no other beer produced by any other brewer which costs so much to brew or age. Our exclusive beech-wood aging provides a taste, a smoothness, and a drinkability that you will find in no other beer at any other price."

If I were acting out the way I felt inside, then I must have felt pretty dirty. To my shame, one day I found Brad's older brother's pornography in his basement, so visits to his house to play billiards sometimes became just a facade as we escaped into the world of *Playboy* and *Penthouse.* Some nights, I would sneak over to Dylan's house to watch whatever soft-core porn we could find on his full-sized satellite dish, even if it were partly scrambled. It was as if I'd become obsessed with behaving badly. As a freshman, when making out with my girlfriend, sex never even entered my mind. Now, it was on my mind *constantly.*

All the partying on the weekends was intended to help me escape my reality, and one of those realities was that I wanted to "get laid." In my pornographic escapes, I was good enough to be with beautiful women. In the real world, I was insecure and lacked the confidence to seduce anyone. Alcohol provided false courage but proved insufficient for meeting my goal.

My drunken pursuits never came to fruition until I set my sights lower. Dylan met a couple of promiscuous younger girls at a party and later had sex with one of them. He made plans for us to double date with them the following week. Dylan assured me I would lose my virginity, and I mistakenly believed I was ready.

The following weekend, we scored some grape MD 20/20, and the four of us decided to park out in the country on an empty lane. We all got drunk. Dylan's car was like two love seats on four wheels; it was huge. So he and his date messed around up front, while my date and I hooked up in the back seat. The whole experience made me feel empty.

Impending Doom

It was springtime, and golf season was in full swing. I was still abusing alcohol regularly, but I was now, at the same time, try-ing to teach a new girlfriend I made about Jesus, the Church of

Christ, and what a great family life looks like. She already believed in Jesus, but she wasn't aware of the "rules" He required. I felt I had a duty before God and the CCOC to show her the way.

One night at the high school's spring luau, I was relieving my bladder when Kevin stepped up to the urinal next to me with some bad news.

"I hate to tell you this, man, but they saw you drinking on the golf course," Kevin reported.

"What?" I barely whispered.

"Yeah, it wasn't so much that you were drinking," he replied. "It just pissed them off that you threw your empties into the lake. They called the school. You'll be called to the office on Monday." And then he promptly walked away.

Only now, because of my profession as a surgeon, can I put into words the way I felt when he told me I had finally been caught. The feeling was a horror akin to when I accidentally nicked the popliteal artery while doing a knee replacement. As blood poured out into a previously dry field, I felt a sinking feeling in the pit of my stomach, my face flushed, and I almost wet my pants. I was overcome with a sense of intense fear and impending doom. After taking control of the situation and getting a vascular surgeon to help me out, I turned to my nurse practitioner and said, "I haven't felt like that since Kevin told me I got caught drinking on the golf course."

My hidden life of debauchery was about to be exposed, so I retreated, sobered up, and rushed home. It was a long night and weekend of ruminating and despairing, but I told no one. My mother was in Kentucky visiting my grandmother, who was dying from Alzheimer's in a nursing home. I worked all day beside my father at the hardware store on Saturday, as usual, and pretended nothing had happened. Then we went to church twice on Sunday as usual. Finally, Monday morning rolled around after a weekend that felt about ten years long.

Lo and behold, Kevin had told the truth. I was sitting in class when I heard it:

"David Hockman, come to the office, please."

Word had gotten around the school, so everyone knew why I was being summoned, which intensified the shame. My arms, legs, and face tingling, I walked down to the office. For such a short walk, I could not believe how short of breath I felt. As I sat in the secretary's office, my heart was racing as fast as my thoughts. I felt like I was locked in a subzero freezer with no hope of escape. My whole body was shivering, and I couldn't understand why. What was happening to me? Was I dying?

Finally, I was called into Vice Principal Roper's office.

As soon as I sat down in the hard, plastic chair across from his desk, he got right to the point. "David, we received a rather troubling call from the staff down at the golf course this morning," he said, his hands folded on the desktop. "It seems you were spotted with alcohol in your possession."

After a three-second attempt at denial, the dam burst, and I confessed. To my surprise, I received a glimmer of grace. Mr. Roper pointed out that the golf course personnel stated that they only saw us in possession of alcohol. They did not report seeing us drinking it. That was enough of a loophole that he was able to limit my expulsion to one week rather than two, thus saving my GPA from a catastrophic decline and preserving my ability to obtain academic scholarships.

I'll never forget his gracious compliment. "David, you're not a bad kid. You've got a good family and a bright future. You made a mistake. Now take this opportunity to live up to your potential."

With those words, I was sent home, assured that a letter explaining my circumstances would be mailed to my parents later. I went straight home and called my father at the store to tell him what happened. My father never closed the store in the middle of a workday, especially with my mom out of town, but as soon as I told him, he locked the door and left.

When he arrived at the house, I confessed to my spring luau sin—but I never confessed to all the sin that had preceded it. He reacted with swift and firm condemnation that cut me to the core and revealed what I had always suspected—you'll never measure up.

"Beer? I can't believe it! Beer!" he chanted over and over, as he stomped his feet, walking a circle from kitchen to dining room to living room and back to the kitchen. "Beer! I can't believe it!"

Finally, he stopped in his tracks and did something I'd never seen him do. In a rage, he turned and punched the microwave, breaking its door. This was back when microwaves were expensive and hard to replace. My next thought was, *Oh sh*t! I hope I'm not next.*

Fortunately, he finally calmed himself and decided on a plan.

"We are not going to tell your mother until she gets back," he said. "But you have to work at the hardware store every day this week so I can keep an eye on you. If anyone asks why you're there, you are to tell them that your dad needed help while your mom was gone."

I asked if I should walk forward at church to confess my public sin, but thankfully, he told me that would not be necessary.

The plan was practical but hypocritical. The CCOC church prescribed a black-and-white formula for life, and Dad's application of the formula seemed highly incongruent. Lie about why I was working? Hide the truth from my mom? Don't follow the "go forward and publicly confess" formula for my publicly committed sin that had brought reproach on the church? It was all wrong. Did that mean I would remain unforgiven? I was confused, but I complied, knowing I had a duty to protect our family's good name.

From Bad to Worse

Sadly, I don't recall a single conversation about any of my feelings or Dad's feelings during that week at work. There seemed to be no concern about why I was acting out. Maybe if I'd had an opportunity to describe my physical symptoms before seeing the vice principal, I could have discovered earlier in life that I'd suffered from a panic attack. Perhaps I could have talked to a doctor or counselor and learned how to manage my undiagnosed anxiety disorder without self-medicating with alcohol.

On Wednesday night, we returned home from church to find that my mother was home early. She had been battling the emotions of caring for her dying mother in a nursing home while also helping her recovering alcoholic father remain home independently on the family farm. She must have been completely drained of energy when she found the school's letter on her dresser bureau.

As soon as she saw me, she commanded me to come into the kitchen and sit down. I complied and sat on the countertop. She then walked up to me and slapped me in the face as hard as she could. My brother later told me he was impressed that I didn't so much as flinch despite the large red handprint on my face. Neither of us had ever been smacked on the face before. We were both shocked. I understood her reaction. Honestly, I was more pissed off by the condemnation and shame than by the assault. Later in my fifties, Mom told me how much she regretted that day.

That night, Dan and I got to hear something new to us: our parents fighting. They'd always claimed they never fought. Now, not only had I condemned myself, but I was guilty of sowing marital discord. From what I could gather, Mom wanted to end my life as I knew it, but Dad wanted to be more lenient. They settled on a one-month grounding, which still allowed my girlfriend to come over.

Despite Vice Principal Roper's grace, in the face of my parents' condemnation, I had little desire to repent. Mom and Dad demanded to know how long I had been drinking, but I didn't trust their motive. Not knowing whether they wanted to help me or condemn me, I assumed the worst and lied to their faces. I did not confess the truth that I had been chronically abusing alcohol for six months. I had driven drunk numerous times as an unlicensed driver. I had blacked out more times than I could recall. And I certainly didn't let them know that I had given up on being the perfect son.

I had also given up on purity with my new girlfriend. We were together almost compulsively. With her as a distraction, I knew I could survive my month-long confinement until I could party again. During that month, my parents seemed to have forgiven me, but I wasn't sure. At least, there were no more slapping or punching appliances. They just went about life as if my expulsion hadn't happened. The only difference was that I did not go out on weekends.

Finally, my confinement ended, and I went out for a sober Friday night only to return home to find Mom and Dad asleep. I woke them up to let them know I was home before the midnight curfew. That was my way of regaining their trust, and it worked. Time to party.

Saturday night, I went out and drank nearly a fifth of vodka. This time, when I returned home at midnight, they were up studying their Sunday school Bible lessons. I tried to hurry past them and go to bed, but Mom asked me to come over and kiss her good night. When I tried to approach her, I stumbled.

"David, you're drunk!" she screamed. "Go to bed!"

They interrogated me, but I refused to reveal the source of my liquor. So my mom stayed up with me all night to ensure I didn't vomit and aspirate. The next morning, she informed me that I had gotten up to pee, walked to the corner of my bedroom, and relieved myself on the carpet. She had to clean both me and the rug. She must have been horrified.

Still a little intoxicated and definitely hungover, I was ordered to get up and get ready for church. As I walked by the hall closet, I noticed a hole in the door. When I discreetly asked my brother about it, he informed me that Dad had punched the door in frustration, and then Mom and Dad had fought most of the night. They fought not only because of me, but also because of Dad's violent reaction, which my mom had never seen before. She had never wanted a home like the one she grew up in, and to my shame, I was providing just that.

My brother Dan took me aside later to talk about how I was living. Of course, I had seen Dan drinking defiantly during high school, and he knew that. But he insisted his drinking was different. Typically, he would split a six-pack with a buddy to get a little buzz, but he never came home intoxicated, which was quite unlike my drinking pattern.

Dan had already helped clean me up a few times when I'd come home wasted and covered in vomit. How my parents never woke up during those late-night clean-ups is beyond me, but Dan cleaned me up and even laundered my clothes without them knowing. Maybe he assumed it was just a few isolated mistakes on my part. Now, however, he knew better and tried to help me. Of course, I was thankful for his enabling my foolishness earlier, but I was more than grateful for his tender concern that morning.

Everyone in the family was hurting because of me. I was hurting too. My parents had chosen to condemn me rather than try to understand the cause of my behavior. I desperately needed them to let down their guard and fearlessly reach out to help me, but they were too afraid and chose to control the situation. They just wanted to know *where* I got the alcohol, not *why* I got it. I needed grace but got shame instead. Still, I knew they were doing the best they could, so after the vodka incident, I decided I would try hard again to walk the straight and narrow path.

Chapter 5

A CCOC DOCTRINAL INTERLUDE

Certain Words

They search the universe,
Gazing at the stars,
Listening to the heavens,
Hoping to find certainty.
When right at our fingertips,
We have the certain words
From prophets long ago,
And we push them aside and never know.
They browse the halls of libraries,
Perusing volumes
Of books and commentaries,
Hoping an answer lies within.
When right at our fingertips
We have the certain words
From prophets long ago,
And we push them aside and never know.

Father give us ears to hear
The words made certain.
Give us hearts that pay attention
To the light shining in a dark place
Until the day dawns and
The morning star
Rises in our hearts.
When rising from our fingertips,
We read from prophets long ago
Certain words of faith, hope, and love,
And we listen and we follow.

I WANT TO STEP away from the narrative briefly to share a little about how I perceived the CCOC doctrine during my childhood, so you can better imagine its impact on my life. Bear in mind that not everyone who attends this denomination is affected the same way I was. It is also true that the CCOC may have changed by the time this book was written. The CCOC has no written creed, so every CCOC member learns the dogma and proof texts by heart. However, I have purposely avoided citing Scripture in this chapter to avoid linking the dignity of Scripture with CCOC dogma.

Old Testament

- God created the world in six literal twenty-four-hour days. If you deny this, you cannot be saved, and the church cannot admit you as a member.

- Adam was the first created human being, and Eve was created to serve and help him, just as a wife is meant to serve and help her husband today.
- If Noah had not built the ark perfectly according to God's instructions, then he would have perished in the flood. Therefore, we have to follow God's instructions perfectly, or we will perish in the fire of Judgment Day.
- Nadab and Abihu offered strange fire to the Lord and were struck dead. Therefore, if we do not worship God exactly as He prescribes, we will be spiritually dead and burn eternally in the afterlife.
- Uzzah unlawfully touched the ark of the covenant and was struck dead. Although God may not strike you dead when you disobey, He still feels the same toward you when you sin as He did toward Uzzah, so follow the rules no matter what.
- David did not sin when he disobeyed God's command and ate the showbread, but if you try to make an excuse for not following the rules, refer back to Nadab, Abihu, and Uzzah. Yes, God preferring mercy to sacrifice is confusing, but err on the side of sacrifice lest you end up like Nadab, Abihu, or Uzzah.
- The Israelites were tragically inept in their ability to follow God. They constantly cycled through obedience, disobedience, punishment, and repentance. They often got what they deserved, so be careful to follow God's law lest you be punished with His harsh discipline, which He will hurl at you out of His love.
- Ultimately, God never forgave the sins of the Israelites until Jesus paid the price with His perfect sacrifice. In Old Testament days, guilt remained on the Israelites until

the annual Day of Atonement sacrifice rolled their sins forward another year. Grace and forgiveness were not present in the Old Testament. That only came with Jesus if you obey Him.

New Testament

- The Sermon on the Mount is to be considered the new law under Christ, even though, oddly enough, all the men in church still have two eyes and two hands. It is intended to be much harder than the old law, but it must be possible to keep it perfectly. Otherwise, Jesus would not have said, "Be perfect, for I am perfect."
- Jesus died to set aside the old covenant and establish a new one, which is good news for non-Jews, who had no hope of reconciliation with God during the time of the old covenant. Now, anyone can become right with God by accepting His gift of grace and following the five-step rules mentioned earlier.
- Jesus's resurrection gives hope to those who remain faithful until His return. Faithfulness is essentially a matter of attending the "one true church" and believing and practicing all that it teaches. Ultimately, your faith saves you from death and gives you eternal life as long as you make sure you have no sins separating you from God at the time of your death. Be sure to repent and ask for forgiveness of your sins as often as you can, because you never know when you might die, and you can never be sure of your salvation.

- Paul's talk of a "sinful nature" in Romans 7 is confusing. We do not have a sinful nature. Everything we do is our explicit, freewill choice, including being saved or lost. So, if you go to hell, it's your own fault, and if you go to heaven, it's because you chose wisely. The Holy Spirit has nothing to do with your salvation other than inspiring the men who wrote the Bible, which tells us what to do to be saved.

- Many Christian hymns give too much confidence in our salvation, so the lyrics must be changed to reflect scriptural truth. For example, in the *Sacred Selections* hymnal, we do not sing "when we all get to heaven" because we cannot be sure that we will all get there. Instead, we sing "when the saved get to heaven." Furthermore, some songs in the hymnal are avoided entirely and should not have been allowed into the canon of the hymnal. For example, "In the Garden" does not belong there because we do not "walk and talk with Jesus," and He certainly doesn't "tell us we are His own." That's just not scriptural.

- Any talk of a "personal relationship with Jesus" is condemned and even belittled because it is not explicitly mentioned word-for-word in the Bible. We are not to buy into this "feelings-based" notion. Jesus is Lord, and you are His subject, so obey.

- Jesus ascended to the right hand of the Father to advocate on our behalf, which means He reminds the Father of His sacrifice on our behalf but only when we pray and ask for forgiveness.

- The Holy Spirit inspired the writers of the Bible, completing His work in our lives. He does not indwell Christians. In reality, the Holy Spirit only figuratively dwells in the hearts of the saved through reading and studying the Scriptures that He inspired. So if you want more of His indwelling, spend more time reading His word. (This notion likely explains why my dad spent so many evenings after dinner in his bedroom reading and studying his Bible, and I'm glad he did because he taught me so much that was good.)

- Just as Noah received a specific pattern for the ark, we have a particular pattern for how to do church. Therefore, you'd better follow it so you don't end up like Ananias and Sapphira, early church members who were struck dead for displeasing God. Concerning corporate worship within the rest of Christendom, their worship is vain.

- The Bible gives three types of authority for the church to follow: direct command, approved example, and necessary inference. Figuring out which examples in the Bible are approved and what to necessarily infer from them isn't easy, and it makes for some good arguments. Still, in the end, the CCOC has book, chapter, and verse for every practice and therefore cannot be questioned since they alone have "no book but the Bible, no creed but Christ." Remember that.

- The Bible tells us to "not be anxious about anything." That is a direct command, so if you worry, that means you are sinning, which implies going to hell unless you repent.

- The apostles and early church met on the first day of the week. Based on this approved example, if you miss corporate worship on Sunday, you are sinning and must repent.

- The early church had communion with bread and wine on the Lord's Day. CCOC infers that communion must be celebrated "every" Sunday, or you are sinning (in which case, yes, you must repent). However, you must keep in mind that New Testament wine was really grape juice, and if you drink wine, you are sinning. Even if it were fermented juice, the alcohol would have been negligible since they diluted it with water.

- If you miss communion on Sunday morning, you'd better show up for the evening service to get your second chance at it (although some CCOC members found this to be an unscriptural practice and refused the evening communion).

- Where the Scriptures are silent, the CCOC claims to be quiet. There is no scriptural authority for things like children's church, staffed nurseries during worship, youth groups, or church family dinners in the church building, so having any of those things is sinful and makes your church "unsound." You may be wondering where the CCOC gets its authority to own a building. After all, the New Testament never instructs Christians to construct church buildings. The answer, of course, is "necessary inference."

- Keep your kids quiet in church. Pinch them, spank them, do whatever you have to do, but for the sake of your own reputation as a good parent, do not let them be disruptive. Everyone is watching and judging your parenting, so parent your kids like the CCOC god parents you.

- The church's treasury is for directly supporting ministers and for helping anyone who is a member of the CCOC. The Scriptures are silent on the church supporting orphanages, Bible schools, religious magazines, parachurch organizations, and helping needy nonchurch members. Therefore, if you support any of these things with church funds, you have an "unsound" church. Refer back to Ananias, Sapphira, Nadab, Abihu, or Uzzah if you think you know better than the CCOC's dogma.

- You'd better not take money from the church treasury to pay for flowers for a member's funeral. Instead, set up a "nonchurch" flower fund. Additionally, potluck church dinners must be held off-site at a rented location, and do not use the church's treasury to pay the rent. Instead, collect the rent from attendees and pay the lessor from that temporary fund. To prove that these funds are not a work of the church, you must never mention them in the opening announcements of corporate worship.

- Man is the head of woman. A woman is a helper of man and must submit to him and remain silent in the church.

- Women cannot teach men. Once a male child is baptized, even if he is ten years of age, a man must take over teaching his class lest the woman teacher be guilty of usurping the authority of the ten-year-old boy.

- Man is the head of the household. Women must be subservient at home.

- Some CCOC men believe a woman must be in subjection to all men, rather than only her husband, and therefore, women should not be leaders in the community or workplace.

- The Bible teaches that there are five items on the checklist for conducting scriptural worship: sing, pray, give, preach, and take communion. I never could figure out where "announcements" fit on that list, but we had them every Sunday and Wednesday.

- The New Testament has passages that command singing, but nothing that explicitly commands or permits the use of instruments. Therefore, all forms of music other than a cappella singing are excluded. A cappella singing is the only music that is acceptable to God. Instrumental worship in "unsound" churches is vain and sinful.

- The Bible commands us not to be "unequally yoked" with nonbelievers, so do not marry or closely associate with anyone outside the CCOC. You can have worldly friends in the other churches, but make sure they do not corrupt you. Also, you should constantly try to convert them to the CCOC. Some, thankfully not Dad, did not believe in reading literature from non-CCOC authors, as that is like drinking water from a poisoned well.

- Always remember that God will hold you accountable for every person you do not share the gospel with, so share Jesus with everyone, or God will be angry with you. (Note: God is always angry with you because no one does this.)
- Last (and only because I have to stop somewhere), never say, "Good grief," because grief is not good, and your speech must be truthful. This point was important enough that I once heard a preacher give an entire sermon about it, so I remember it well. My parents thought the lesson was as ridiculous as I did.

In summary, if there is any way to make a person feel like they can never be fully reconciled to God, or if there is any way to minimize grace and emphasize man's work in being reconciled to God, then the CCOC has likely taught such a belief. Of course, that is hyperbole, but that is often how I felt and interpreted what I was taught.

Certainly, things change over time, and the dogma that I grew up with may have softened among some congregations (and hardened in others). Without denominational leadership, each CCOC congregation set its own tone, often leading to fighting between congregations, which were aired out in magazines such as *Searching the Scriptures* or *Truth*, to which our family had long-standing subscriptions.

Now, back to our story.

Chapter 6

A SOBER UPPERCLASSMAN

Face-to-Face

When I look into God's Eyes
Will I lie about who He sees?
Is it Jesus Christ my Savior?
Or is it only me?

Am I sorry that I've been caught?
Will I stop because of pride?
Or will my heart be shaped and molded
Into the image of Christ?

Let the time of refreshing come
Shower me with your grace
Overflow within my heart
Love me face-to-face

> Bring me back to Eden
> Fully in Your Presence
> Seeing Jesus in me
> Love me face-to-face

I WAS CONVINCED ALL my teachers and coaches thought that I was a loser, so I tried hard to prove them wrong. After my expulsion and vodka drama, I spent the remainder of my sophomore year in repentance, resolving to be a better person. In time, I finally regained my parents' trust. My junior and senior years were going to be successful.

This was easier said than done, particularly on the field. High school sports brought the typical small-town drama, especially for an average athlete like me. I played multiple sports but didn't really excel at any of them. In football, I was disappointed when I didn't start on the O-line as a junior, so I didn't play my senior year. I finally made the varsity wrestling team my junior year at the 160-pound weight class, only to miss the entire season due to an appendectomy. Golf was much better sober, though I struggled to maintain a spot as the fifth man on the varsity team. Maybe sports just weren't my thing. I seemed much more suited for the concert choir and swing choir. In fact, the timeline of the varsity letters I received probably says a lot about me: academics first, then choir, then sports.

Actually, the most impactful part of my upperclassman years happened not in school but in church. Our church had gotten too small to offer a high school class, so I graduated to the adult class on Sunday mornings and Wednesday nights. I became like a fly on the wall, listening to the deranged classroom conversations of my spiritual abusers but saying little.

We would go through books of the Bible verse by verse. Teachers included my father and other churchmen. None of these people had any seminary training, nor did they have a written creed on what the Church of Christ believed, yet somehow they had virtually the same answers to all the major issues listed earlier. Their class "discussions" only increased my doubts about the "one true church."

A simple example is the issue of marriage, divorce, and remarriage. The topic comes up in the four Gospels and in the books of Romans and First Corinthians, so it was discussed frequently. I understood that God wanted marriage to be for life, but I didn't understand the CCOC belief about how God views divorced couples. For divorcées, CCOC classes were filled with accusations, judgment, and, of course, a strict formula for them to follow.

According to CCOC teaching, if a man and woman divorced for any reason other than adultery, then they were not allowed ever to get married again to anyone else except the former spouse. Unless there was reconciliation, they had to stay unmarried. If they did remarry someone other than their former spouse, even if they were faithful to their new spouse, they were considered guilty of perpetual, unrepentant adultery and, therefore, destined for hell.

On the other hand, according to the CCOC formula, if you are the non-adulterous party in an adulterous marriage, then you can remarry. If you are the guilty party, you may never remarry another person lest you be eternally condemned due to the unrepentant, perpetual adultery in your life. The only option for guilty divorcées, whether it's guilt by adultery or guilt by divorcing for another cause, is to remarry the original spouse or remain celibate.

What if you found yourself in a failed marriage due to physical abuse, abandonment, or some other awful thing besides adultery? Since you would be facing a potentially unforgivable sin, wouldn't it be wiser to murder the spouse and repent by never murdering again? (My conclusion, not the church's.) Then you would be free to remarry because death severs the marital bond. Could God be so cruel?

CCOC cruelty extends even further. If a non-Christian couple, who were both previously married, divorced, and now remarried, visits the CCOC and later decides to become Christians, they have to follow the five steps. Unless both were innocent victims of adulterous former spouses, then to repent (step three), they would be told to divorce. That's the only way they could go to heaven. That is not hyperbole. It's not just a hypothetical. I've seen it happen to a couple who had children living in their home. It seems the remedy to the problem of marriage, divorce, and remarriage was divorce. You can understand why I found it all so confusing. Can you imagine the confusion of the children whose parents suddenly divorced?

Shame or Suffering

A more complex example of how Sunday morning and Wednesday evening class discussions fed my doubts about the CCOC arises from a criminal matter with our preacher. Evidently, the preacher had been physically abusing his wife, and when she'd finally had enough, she called the police. Believe it or not, her behavior was considered questionable by some members, for two reasons. First, the Bible states that a brother should not take a brother to court, as it would bring shame on the church. Some of the men in the Sunday morning class expected the wife to let the church handle her marital strife internally. Second, they questioned whether she erred by being unwilling to suffer abuse for the sake of Christ.

The class spent a surprising amount of time deliberating this issue. Thankfully, I heard my father defend the woman's action as necessary to protect herself and her children. I think his defense helped me disassociate my father's teaching from the CCOC's. The noticeable difference between my father and the other men in the CCOC was confusing but comforting.

I certainly respected Dad more than the other argumentative CCOC men. In general, my father was genuinely happy and seemed most Christlike when he was taking Dan or me to a widow's house to fix a screen or change a furnace filter. He was often smiling, singing, or whistling. He had joy in his walk with God, but for the life of me, I could not figure out why.

Ironically, the CCOC's notion that the elders of the church should be called rather than the police in civil disputes was not possible because, to my knowledge, the churches I grew up in never had any elders. We could never agree on having any men who perfectly met the biblical qualifications for eldership. There is a saying that God doesn't call the qualified but qualifies the called. We seemed to believe more in a God who disqualifies than in one who calls.

The CCOC men's mode of operation was to elevate all men together rather than separating out some as leaders. Even so, the highest achievement for all good CCOC men was to become an elder. A woman, of course, could never be considered for eldership. Since women were to be silent in church, they were not welcome at men's business meetings.

These nonsensical CCOC judgments turned me off, but I figured if this was the "one true church," then I had nowhere else to go. Ultimately, adult classes did more to drive a wedge between God and me than to grow my faith. More than ever, the God of the CCOC seemed angry and anxious to condemn.

Unfortunately, CCOC's view of women as lesser beings worked its way into our home. It's hard to imagine a time before television remote controls. Still, it's even harder to imagine a boy calling his mom into the living room to change the channel for him while she is in the kitchen preparing his dinner. However, that's precisely what happened in my home. My brother and I would call our mother into the room, no matter what she was doing, to bring us iced tea, to turn up the volume, or to bring us snacks. And my mother would rush in to wait on us. She truly had a servant's heart in our home.

This situation didn't change until one day, when my brother's girlfriend, Rebekah, was present and witnessed it. As my mother ran in to change the channel, Rebekah was astonished, outraged, and just plain pissed to see how Mom was treated. And she let us know it. As strange as it may seem, it had never dawned on us that we were being misogynistic pigs. Dan and I certainly didn't want to be that way. Honestly, we didn't know any better, as our father would often do the same.

Rebekah opened our eyes to the reality of this mistreatment of women. After that, I began to wonder what else we were missing by growing up in the sheltered, exclusive CCOC way. Looking back, I'm thankful to Rebekah for teaching us to treat women better, and I'm sure she's grateful as well, since she has been married to Dan for thirty-six years.

Moral and Spiritual Confusion

Despite my newfound desire to treat women better, I still failed to honor women sexually. I put my desires above God's desires. The constant shame of knowing that God would never be happy with me and never save me until I conquered this sin wore me down. Over and over, I'd try hard to repent, only to give up again. I constantly battled stomach pains and had difficulty falling asleep, likely due to the anxiety that comes with intense shame.

The one reprieve from my moral and spiritual confusion occurred at a Fellowship of Christian Athletes (FCA) concert event in Kansas City. Technically, I was not allowed to join the FCA because they were not Christians according to the CCOC. However, I was invited to the concert and attended out of curiosity. The vocal and instrumental music combined in such a moving way that I felt drawn closer to God, yet I was supposed to believe that instrumental worship was condemned. According to the CCOC, what I was feeling was just an emotional high and had nothing to do with my spiritual condition, but I loved it.

After that concert, I desperately wanted to change for the better, to give up my head-banging heavy metal, to be chaste, and ultimately to have what they had at FCA: a real, personal relationship with Jesus. As far as I knew from past teaching, my desire for change could only be fueled by my will, which had constantly cycled through trying hard and giving up. Everything seemed to return to normal after a few days, but during that brief time of "enlightenment," I caught a glimpse of grace only to be too fearful to receive it.

My efforts in school far exceeded my efforts in morality. When I finally graduated from high school, it brought a welcome relief from my efforts to prove that all the teachers and coaches were wrong about me. I'd spent two years walking the halls of OGHS in mint green high-top Converse tennis shoes, with a chip on the shoulder of my heavy metal concert T-shirt, but I somehow managed to get good letters of recommendation. The Army and Air Force both offered me full-ride ROTC Scholarships to any college in the United States, and I was accepted to my dream school, Washington University in St. Louis. Sadly, Washington was too expensive for ROTC to cover more than 75 percent of the tuition, but the university respected the ROTC scholarship and awarded me the remaining 25 percent as a scholarship.

Believe it or not, I turned down *both* of the scholarships. First of all, my family could not afford the $8,000 per year room and board at Washington University, and we did not qualify for a government loan despite being lower-middle-class. Second, ROTC would not guarantee that I could go straight to medical school after college. In hindsight, I realize that if I had taken the scholarship, I would likely have served in Operation Desert Storm rather than going straight to medical school. Last, when I visited the Washington University campus, I saw all the BMWs and Mercedes in the student parking lot and felt like a hillbilly who didn't belong.

My self-esteem was low despite my academic accomplishments, mostly because I knew that God was not pleased with me. The truth is that I was never satisfied with myself either. No matter how hard I tried, I seemed to fall short of both my expectations and His. So it was fitting that I did not get valedictorian, despite taking four years of science and math and having perfect grades. Instead, I was the salutatorian behind someone who had one more A than I did because of her band classes. Fortunately, I soon qualified for two full-tuition scholarships to UMKC, along with an additional $3,500 per year. That made up for second place. I realize now that without those scholarships, I would not be where I am today. While the money had an immense impact on my life, my low self-esteem didn't leave me much room for celebration. I just moved on to the next goal. No accomplishment could change the fact that I was deeply ashamed of who I was.

College and medical school lay before me, and I was ready to go it alone, depending on the only one whom I could trust—me. I never once prayed about God's will for my future. It never dawned on me to do anything other than tell God my plans and ask Him to bless them. I knew what I wanted in life, and nothing and no one was going to stand in my way.

I wanted to be a successful, respected physician who helped people as I had been helped. As I mentioned, I was frequently ill during first grade, but I also made several trips to the doctor every year for abdominal pain, headaches, or sinus issues. Each time, Dr. Deniro or Dr. Giovanni would find a way to help me. They seemed to get me and knew that my stress level was intolerable. Mentally, I'm sure they realized something was going on, something was causing all of my stress, but the closest they ever came to commenting on my mental health was to say that I was "just a little high-strung."

Not only was I impressed with their ability to help me over the years, but I knew that if I achieved their level of success, I wouldn't have to worry about eating ground beef for days on end because money was tight and business was slow.

Chapter 7

MY GREATEST GIFT

A Gift of Grace

I saw you today
Out of the corner of my eye
I looked at you as you looked away

You looked so pretty
Dancing in the middle of Broadway
In a downtown parade

We crossed paths today
At the drug store
Getting sodas for a treat

Your arm brushed against mine
I blushed
And looked at you as you looked away

Our hometown beat yours in ball today
I cheered against you
As I sat next to another

You looked so beautiful
Running up and down the court
And you looked at me as I looked away

We met for the first time today
You were glamorous and tan
Waiting for me at the lake

I walked past you
As you teasingly ignored me
And I looked at you and you looked at me

We spent the summer together
Everyday was blessed
By your charm and grace

We kissed and cuddled
We exchanged "I love you"
As I looked at you and you looked at me

You gave yourself to me today
I was enraptured by your touch
You were perfect and pure

Yet, you wondered about another
Though she was long forgotten
I looked at you as you looked away

I should have saved myself for you.

FLUSH WITH CASH from graduation and free from any responsibility, the summer after my senior year became the best season of my life. Time stood still as I took it all in, pondered it, and rejoiced.

The goal was freedom and independence. Ready to take on the world, I had signed a lease to live on my own in an apartment in Kansas City. The plan was to move out in August and continue the journey toward becoming a physician. Before that deadline, I intended to enjoy life with my guy friends.

And then providence upended my summer agenda. One evening, I got a call from Clay, who was working at Lake Paradise with my best friends Dylan and Brad.

"You remember the Massey twins from Odessa? We used to cheer against them at the girls' volleyball and basketball games?" he asked.

"Which twin?" I asked.

"The tall one with the big hair," he replied.

"Yeah, I guess so. Why?" I responded. Actually, I recalled several good-looking girls on the Bulldog teams.

"Well, her mom is an English teacher at our school," Clay continued.

"And?"

"And she thinks you and Grant Tull are hot, so I said I'd try to set her up. Get this: She's a virgin."

"So what am I supposed to do?" I asked.

"Call her. Here is her number."

I was not confident with the opposite sex, so I was stunned by what I did next. Throwing caution to the wind, I called the girl as soon as I hung up with Clay. I don't know what I was thinking. I suppose I wasn't thinking. If I had been, fear would have taken over. "Hello?" someone answered. A man's voice.

"Yes, may I speak to Sherry Massey, please?" I replied.

"Sure, just a second," he said as he went to find her.

A moment later, she spoke.

"Hello?"

"Hi, this is David Hockman. Clay said you'd like to go out with me sometime," I proudly proclaimed, as if I had done this sort of thing many times before.

"Oh. Yeah, OK," she said, laughing nervously. Unbeknownst to me, this was totally out of character for her, too.

"How about a movie Saturday night?"

"Well, I work until eight o'clock."

"That's fine. I'll pick you up at Lake Paradise when you get off work."

"OK, see you then."

"OK, goodbye."

"Goodbye."

We hung up, and I couldn't believe what had just happened. We had only agreed to a date. Neither of us wanted to enter college in a committed relationship. We both wanted freedom, but again, Providence knew better.

The date almost didn't happen, but I'm forever grateful that it did. I had a summer cold and was going to cancel the date, but my dad encouraged me to go anyway.

"You never know what may come of it," he foreshadowed.

That evening, Sherry and I watched *Roadhouse* with Patrick Swayze. Later, she tried to kiss me goodnight, but I turned away to spare her my contagion. On the drive home, I realized she'd left her backpack in my car that night.

Smooth move, Sherry, I thought, but she later denied that it was intentional.

We both spoke separately to our mutual friend, Clay, and our comments about each other were the same: "He/she has the most beautiful big brown/blue eyes." The compliment was a nice change, since I had been frequently made fun of over the years for having "bug" eyes. Even my best friend would tease me by calling me Gollum from *The Lord of the Rings*. We were captivated by each other, and I couldn't wait to feel better, so I could return her backpack and see her again.

One week later, I drove out to her house to return her backpack. I was nervous to meet her family, so I brought a buddy with me. Sherry's family members weren't strangers to me. Her three siblings worked out at Lake Paradise with some of my friends, and my friends enjoyed working with them. Plus, I already knew Sherry's mom from school, but I was still nervous. We've only had one date, after all.

It was a brilliant day, full of sunshine and warmth. We drove out in the country for what seemed like forever. We finally arrived at the top of a hill, overlooking forty acres filled with cattle and horses and Sherry's big brick house. She answered the door in a T-shirt and men's boxer shorts. Her skin was tan from lifeguarding. She needed little to no makeup to look just as stunning as she did on our first date. After visiting for an hour, we made plans for a second date.

Sherry and I wound up spending the entire summer together. We went to Worlds of Fun, Oceans of Fun, Starlight Theatre, the movie theater, the Kansas City Zoo, Nelson-Atkins Museum of Art, multiple shopping malls, Country Club Plaza, and Lake Jacomo. We ate at every style of restaurant we could think of. I could go on and on. Suffice it to say, we spent all of my graduation money without regret.

We were falling in love quickly. Our first date was June 17, and by July 8, we had professed our love and committed to seeing each other exclusively. It was the happiest summer of our lives.

Looking back, I know now that the call from Clay was a special act of grace from my loving Father God. As it turned out, Sherry had been looking through her mom's copy of my high school yearbook when she came across a picture of me in an acid-washed jean jacket. She thought I was attractive, and, in a bold, uncharacteristic act, she mentioned it to Clay. Sherry asking Clay to set her up was every bit as spontaneous and bold as me calling her and asking for a date. We had both taken a chance and were unexpectedly surprised by the outcome.

God's providence was not something the CCOC spent much time talking about. To them, life was what you made of it through your own efforts and merit. To me, it all seemed like chance and hormones at the time, but now I know better. God knew precisely what Sherry and I needed, and He loved us so much that He used a yearbook photograph and our mutual friend Clay to give it to us.

I wish I still had that jean jacket.

Chapter 8

BACK TO REALITY

In You

When I am afraid,
When I feel alone,
When I can't go on,

You comfort me
With Your holy
Presence

Your Spirit
Within
Prays for me

And I know
I can trust
In You.

ONCE IT BECAME clear to our parents that we were seriously committed to our summer romance, they each had a warning for us. Sherry's parents cautioned her that CCOC boys only marry CCOC girls. My parents expressed concern for Sherry's lost Baptist soul. We each had a dilemma. Sherry had to decide whether she could put up with someone so narrow-minded, and I had to decide whether I could convert her. Thankfully, she was pretty easy-going, and I was willing to take a chance.

With the best summer ever behind us, we headed our separate ways to college. I went to the University of Missouri-Kansas City, and she headed to William Jewel in Liberty, Missouri. I got my own apartment, while she shared a dorm room with her best friend. Her older brother was playing basketball at Jewell, so she instantly had a community. I, on the other hand, felt isolated and knew no one. This depressing transition of mine was manageable only because of Sherry.

We kept the road hot between us. The forty-five-minute drive was tough on those nights when we stayed out late. In fact, I nearly crashed twice before setting a rule that we had to part company by ten o'clock each night. Our relationship quickly developed enough depth that we were convinced we would one day marry. Being in her presence filled me with a peaceful happiness that promptly dissipated in her absence. At a time in my life when I could have been learning to depend on God, I was instead becoming dependent on the one person God was counting on me to convert to His "one true church." But what if I failed to change her?

Ironically, Sherry and I began having Bible studies together around the same time we started having sex. My heart's desire was for her soul to be saved, but my carnal desire was for her to give me pleasure. It was a confusing time to mix deep intimacy with hellfire-and-brimstone preaching. In retrospect, the hypocrisy of it all was shameful. I was a parody of Christianity, polished and shiny on the outside but filthy on the inside.

Like a good little CCOC boy, I continued to attend my parents' church through the first two years of college. Sherry joined me each time, driving miles and miles to worship at the altar of the "one true church" like a dedicated disciple. After my weekends with Sherry, the rest of my week was filled with perfectionism and self-flagellation. Making A's in college did not make up for my moral failure, and my deep love for Sherry did not make up for my shame. I didn't realize it at the time, but I was sinking into depression brought on by cognitive dissonance.

Conversion and Conflict

One dreary morning after class, I arrived at my apartment to the sight of two fire engines and a sea of red foam. Firefighters were cleaning up a rather large pool of blood left by my neighbor who lived across the hall. She had jumped from the eleventh floor to her death that morning while I was in class. I didn't know her, but we had crossed paths in the hallway. Still, my sadness at her suicide was compounded by the CCOC teaching that she was certainly now in hell since her last act was to murder herself. Based on their legalistic doctrine, her condemnation was assured. However, from a human standpoint, since I didn't know what her struggles were or what illness she might've had, it made no sense for me to condemn her.

Despite this internal struggle with doubt, which I quietly pushed to the back of my mind, I had an intense motivation to show Sherry "the Way, the Truth, and the Life" that came only through the CCOC. I desperately needed her to accept that she was not saved, that her childhood baptism was invalid, and that her whole family was in danger of hell's fire. Her conversion could save her entire family from an eternity of suffering if they, too, saw the light. God was depending on me to convince her, and I loved her too much to "agree to disagree." Somehow, I had to convince her that a CCOC baptism was the exact moment when a child of the devil becomes a child of God. I had to take control of this situation to ensure our destiny together.

Chef Boyardee pizza was a family favorite back then, so I would make a pizza, wrap it in aluminum foil, and drive up to William Jewell every week for a Bible study with Sherry. We would read the Bible together, and I would show her passages that seemed to prove my point, regardless of the context. Her soul and our future depended on this. We went round and round, arguing in circles about the supreme importance of baptism until finally, in October 1989, during our first year, she asked me to baptize her "in the name of the Father, Son, and Holy Spirit for the remission of sins."

It was a glorious day, but honestly, I now feel ashamed that I spiritually abused her into submission to a false doctrine. In retrospect, the things I taught her were so disgusting that I cannot believe she stayed with me. I actually told her that unless she accepted that her family, both living and dead, were going to hell for being Baptists, then she could not be rebaptized because she would not have entirely accepted the importance of salvation by baptism. Thankfully, from her perspective, she was merely owning her faith in Jesus as an adult, and she never actually bought into all the CCOC dogma.

Her family was not pleased with her decision, especially since they were not invited to the baptism. After Sherry's re-baptism, her family became even more suspicious of me and our relationship. They believed I was too controlling. I can't imagine why. All I wanted was for their daughter to think exactly like me, act exactly like me, and believe exactly like me. The more they fought against us, the more I dug my heels in, with Sherry serving as the rope in our tug of war.

Why she stayed with me through all of this is truly perplexing. Later, when I asked her about this, she reassured me that she knew I had a good heart. Sherry said she loved me and wanted to be with me in a peaceful relationship, unlike what her parents had. She put up with her father sabotaging her car so she would miss Sunday mornings with me. She tolerated her mother diving across a bed at her in anger, only to help her mother up after she fell. At least they both laughed about that.

We wanted to be together constantly. When family trips came up on both sides, we wanted to go together, which only added to the friction. Sherry would come to me for comfort about her parents' treatment, and I would add to her misery by attacking her parents. My immaturity, controlling nature, and selfishness should have repulsed her, but for some reason, she accepted me despite myself.

We were so determined to be together all the time that we decided that we needed to attend the same university. UMKC made the most sense because William Jewell was more expensive. So she transferred over for our sophomore year. Though we technically lived separately, we took turns fixing dinner for each other and enjoying the privacy of my studio apartment. Our relationship grew closer and more comfortable, though still marred by sin.

A Drug for My Doubts

Sherry and I continued attending the same CCOC whenever the doors were open, which meant seeing my parents two or three times a week. On the outside, my life was still too closely tied to theirs, but on the inside, I was becoming curious about life beyond the CCOC way. Joining the University Singers choir put me in contact with people from all walks of life, and I found their stories and behavior intriguing and strange. Writing songs, studying music, smoking pot, dropping acid, throwing lingerie parties, and listening to the Doors opened up a whole new world to me that certainly did not align with the CCOC way of thinking.

Being a righteous conservative on his way to medical school was starting to feel overwhelming, and I wondered if my choir buddies had a better take on life. Vacillating between enjoying a little alcohol to relax and being a good CCOC teetotaler only brought on more anxiety and shame. The occasional private stress relief of pornography didn't soothe my hellbent pursuit of perfection. It only brought even more shame. Migraines and stomach pain became the norm, as I began to wonder who I truly was and what I was meant to become.

I knew a better life must be out there, but I also knew I would be damned if I found it. When I was feeling particularly discouraged, I would daydream about becoming a choir conductor or music teacher. After reading Jim Morrison's biography, I wondered how free my mind would be if I dropped acid like he did. And as I rehearsed Mahler's Eighth Symphony at the Community of Christ auditorium in Independence, I wondered if I'd feel freer if I smoked dope during our breaks like my choir friends did.

One night before going to the movie *The Doors*, I secretly tried pot, but it had no effect. Evidently, like President Bill Clinton, I did not know how to inhale and get the drug deep in my lungs where it could be absorbed. That night at the movie, I saw a family from church and was scared to death that I reeked of marijuana. It ruined my night. Not only was I not high, but I was sure I would get busted again for being less than who I was supposed to be.

That fear never came to fruition, but I did learn that my curiosity about dope was sated enough to prevent further experimentation. Additionally, the movies they'd shown us in sixth grade of kids jumping off buildings, thinking they could fly, because of the effects of LSD, were too powerfully stuck in my mind to allow any further drug use. But mostly, I didn't want to disappoint Sherry with the truth about my curiosity. She didn't learn about my one-time pot use before *The Doors* movie until fifteen years later.

A Fresh Start

Wanting a fresh start and higher-quality teaching, Sherry and I decided to attend the University of Missouri-Columbia together in the fall of our junior year. We had created some great memories together in Kansas City, but it was time to put some distance between our parents and us. By the end of our sophomore year, there was so much conflict in Sherry's home over me that she moved in with my family during the summer one month before our junior year. Her family even staged an intervention with her one night in an effort to keep her out of what they believed was a cult.

Sherry's moving out made it clear that she was not going to give in. Even so, she was not necessarily giving in to the CCOC way either, though neither her parents nor I knew that at the time. In truth, by God's grace, Sherry just wanted to be with me and be at peace with her parents.

Fortunately, shortly before our move to Columbia, Sherry and her family reconciled. It was great timing since I had decided to propose to her in the fall. I actually decided that summer. While taking a break from floating on the Niangua River, I enjoyed the rope swing for about a half an hour before convincing Sherry to try it. She did it once, but then she said she would rather watch me. What surprised me was that she meant what she said. She wasn't just saying the right thing like every CCOC man expects from a woman. Sherry truly found joy in my happiness.

I made up my mind that day that I would propose to her at that exact spot one day that fall. That day came in October 1991.

Chapter 9

A New Beginning with New Friends

Sanctify Me

Father, how do You tolerate us?
We seem unable to learn,
Making the same mistakes
time and again.
Yet You so loved us
That You gave us
Your only Son.

Father, why do we do it?
Repeatedly abusing
Your Spirit's temple,
We indulge and suffer.
Yet, if we believe in You,
We will not die
But live eternally.

Father, will You help us?
Will you shape and mold us
Into the likeness
Of Your Beloved Son
And complete in us
The work You have begun?

AFTER LIVING BY myself for two years, I shared a prison-cell-sized room with someone that the residency coordinator assigned to me before the days of computer matching software. He was about six feet three inches tall and weighed 250 pounds, with long black hair and a matching full beard that reached his chest. To say he was scary-looking doesn't quite capture the picture I saw when I entered the room and first laid eyes on him. He blankly stared into space, planted at a tiny desk, with soft music playing in the background as he clipped a coil of heavy-gauge metal wire into C-shaped rings. This was my introduction to LARPing, also known as live-action role-playing. He was clipping rings to make a suit of chain mail armor for group medieval reenactments.

I thought that if I moved into a dorm, I could make friends more easily, but I was wrong. Transitioning from the independence of apartment life to communal dorm life as an upperclassman was like driving down the interstate in reverse. While I was busy preparing for marriage, the kids in my hall were struggling to figure out life away from their mommies. The maturity gap between us was too wide a gap to form meaningful friendships.

As I got to know my LARPer roomie, I found him tolerable and pleasant enough, until he started playing volleyball every night without showering and brought the stench back to our prison cell. For a few nights, I tried spraying Lysol in his direction at night to keep the smell at bay. It was rude and ineffective.

Students were supposed to give the roommate experience a few weeks before requesting a change, but I couldn't wait. Thankfully, my RA understood my situation and made an exception.

My next roommate was a St. Louis richie-rich boy, who didn't know how to iron his own clothes. Ralph Lauren long-sleeve oxfords, short-sleeve polos, and khakis filled his closet. Like the LARPer, he was nice enough, but when the porn tapes started showing up weekly, along with a blow-up sex doll, I asked to move to a private room during the semester break. My parents were gracious enough to pay the extra fee.

I did manage to make a few acquaintances on our dorm floor. They were former high school golfers from near Oak Grove, who remembered my team as a bunch of cheaters. Naturally, I responded to their accusation with a lie of righteous indignation. They didn't give up easily, but I stuck to my false story.

The only true friendship lay within the confines of the CCOC. Sherry and I made many friends at the only sound church in Columbia, Missouri. Since the CCOC didn't have college ministers, the leaders within the congregation took an interest in us. There were fifteen to twenty college kids in the congregation, and we frequently got together for food and games at the homes of older members.

Strangely enough, I don't recall ever having a Bible study as part of these gatherings. Unlike the campus ministries, we kept to ourselves. Our fellowship stayed on a surface level, stuck in the shallow realm of news, weather, and sports, as we maintained our masks of righteousness with each other. Our version of friendship had no room for deep trust.

Many of these masks were involuntarily removed later in life, revealing various hidden sins. Two members were later caught with pornography on their computers at work and fired. At least one had an adulterous affair. One resigned from his job due to a sexual harassment allegation. Another nearly went bankrupt. All were decent people, but they had real problems and never felt safe enough in the CCOC environment to reveal their deepest, darkest secrets and seek help. I was no different. I would rather have died than admit that I enjoyed alcohol in moderation. And I definitely would have rather been tortured and imprisoned in a dog cage for decades than confess to sexual sin.

Leveled Up Legalism

The local CCOC on the north side of town was especially adept at portraying what they imagined a faithful follower of Christ should look like. We dressed up for worship because casual dress was disrespectful to Jesus. We arrived on time to show proper respect for God. The lights were dimmed to signal when it was time to sit down and get somber for worship. Once seated, you stayed seated. Exiting the sanctuary during a song, prayer, or Scripture reading was a slap in the face of the Almighty.

We were constantly trying to improve our vocal performance during a cappella worship. They even offered singing classes. We learned shape notes so that even nonmusically trained people could hit every note. God deserved our best in everything, especially our worship in song. In fact, the best Christians all attended music classes so they could become more pleasing to God by developing their vocal prowess. Melody may come from the heart, as the Bible says, but we never let that get in the way of a perfect four-part harmony. We were sure that if visitors came into our church and heard our choral abilities, the sweet aroma of Christ would flow into their ears and draw them to the Lord. And that was virtually the only extent to which we were evangelical.

To their credit, this church did take care of its own with fierce devotion. When I came down with the stomach flu, one of the elder's wives offered to take me into their home and nurse me back to health. That seemed like an amazing sacrifice. Who chooses to bring vomit and diarrhea into their home except someone touched by grace?

The best thing that happened to me at our new church was meeting Darius, who was a decade ahead of me in pursuing a medical career. He and his wife, Jada, became good friends with Sherry and me. Over Sunday night pizza at their place, we had many conversations about the road ahead. Darius had chosen orthopaedic surgery partly because he had enjoyed his summer construction jobs so much. The day he allowed me to watch him perform a total hip replacement at the VA hospital changed my life. I was blown away that doctors could use the same tools I sold at my dad's hardware store to help people walk. That began my interest in orthopaedics.

Work Buddies

By far the most fun I had with friends was the time I spent with my coworkers at Arkansas Freightways. My brother worked for the company in Kansas City and recommended me for a job in Columbia. I worked from 5:00 p.m. to 10:00 p.m., Monday through Friday, and the pay was great. Even better were the people. They were humble and kind, hard-working people who were far more like me than the yuppies in college. All of us dockworkers and drivers got along great and enjoyed many Friday nights drinking beers together. We'd sit on a tailgate just off the company's property line or go to a local hole-in-the-wall bar. I felt like I could be my genuine self around these people without all the pretending.

The work was hard, but it was worth it. When the weather got hot and humid, I would come home to the dorm drenched in sweat, with my jeans completely soaked through. When it was cold, I still managed to sweat beneath my generic off-brand Carhartts. The nights when I mainly operated a forklift were the best. We had music blaring from the speakers, forever binding my good memories of '90s country to my time working the docks. Best of all, I was earning the money that Sherry and I would depend on later as a young married couple. I even stayed in town over the summer to continue working and saving for our future.

That summer apart would be followed by our together forever, which began on August 8, 1992.

Chapter 10

Holy Matrimony

Our Life

Our life together is like
Calm peaceful waters
Deep with tranquility
Covered with the breath of God

The sunlight dancing across the waves
Fills me with the joy we have known

Your eyes on our wedding day
Your smile at the birth of our children
Your embrace each day of our lives together

In your presence, I am breathless
With you, I am at home

You are everything to me

The warmth of an open fire
On a serene autumn night
Illuminating the colors

The beauty of God's creation
From the pinnacle of mountains
To ivory shores by the sea

The love that keeps a newborn
Carefully swaddled in a soft quilt
And held cheek to cheek

You are my salvation
From life's lonely sentence

Our life together
Is my most cherished gift from God

HOW COULD SOMEONE who knew so much about me still love me enough to marry me? It sounds pathetic, and I *was* pathetic in my own eyes. Pathetic for hiding my anxiety, shame, and sin behind a mask of confidence and self-righteousness. What did I not know about her? Did it matter? I had found the one for whom my heart longed, someone who accepted me along with my doubts and fears. In turn, she had found in me the one who lifted her up and made her feel secure, confident, and safe.

In His kindness, God blessed us with each other. And so, on a beautiful sunny day in August, we vowed before Him in the

First Baptist church "to have and to hold, from this day forward, for better, for worse, for richer, for poorer, in sickness and in health, to love and to cherish, till death do us part."

The day was as perfect as we could have expected. Sherry radiated inner beauty in her sequined, silhouette-cut, white wedding gown with full-length sleeves, puffy, cloud-like shoulders, and a long, flowing train. She was stunning. As she walked down the aisle to me, I saw her like never before. The look on my face brought tears to her mother's eyes. However, the wedding photos from that day reveal that her father did not share the tender emotions. In every picture, he appears stone cold and stoic because, in his mind, the cult had won. The CCOC had wooed his daughter away from the faith.

I had a lot to prove to him before I would gain his acceptance. Nonetheless, the day was nearly perfect and marked the beginning of a deeper friendship and closeness between Sherry and me than I ever could have imagined.

Two Hitched Hicks

Our marriage started as most do, floating on cloud nine. As two hicks from small towns, we honeymooned where we could get the cheapest flights and hotel rooms, which at the time was Daytona Beach. Each of us had only been on an airplane once before. I can still see her long curly hair pulled back in a low ponytail and the pink lipstick on her tanned face as we boarded the plane.

Staying in a hotel seemed like a luxury to us. When we discovered a jetted tub, we sat in it in our swimsuits to take pictures. To save money on breakfast, we ate from a long tube of miniature powdered donuts and drank Pepsi from a two-liter bottle.

On the way home, we ran out of cash and had to share our last purchase: a single-scoop ice cream cone. I thought she hogged it all; she thought I did.

We came home to a two-bedroom apartment in a semi-safe part of town. The rent was only $200 a month, but we got what we paid for. To get into the bathroom, we had to turn our shoulders sideways. The refrigerator was harvest gold, and the oven was avocado green. The neighbors downstairs had a baby and fought constantly. We heard everything.

At the time, Sherry worked at JCPenney, waited tables at the Country Club of Columbia, and did real estate telemarketing. I continued at what became American Freightways. All the while, both of us were full-time students. Our schedules were busy, but it was the best year of college.

Chapter 11

MED SCHOOL DRAMA

Preparing for Finals

Overtaken by loneliness,
I sit at my desk to study.
Peering out the window,
Watching life pass away.
The leaves have all fallen, and
I've only just begun.
Life is but a vapor!
Am I certain of my choices?
Will life's end bring regrets?
Will I rue my day of admission?
My wife, I never see.
She, too, has made choices.
What will our end be?
Two separate lives,
I had not envisioned.

United in marriage,
Separated by choices.
Are we certain of those choices?

STARTING MEDICAL SCHOOL was the culmi-
nation of years of hard work in high school and college. I
was young and idealistic, and my path was simultaneously
thrilling and terrifying. My restless soul had arrived at the launch
point of proving my worth in life.

The medical school used a problem-based learning curriculum,
which placed us in small groups throughout the first two years.
As a class, we were close-knit. Our new curriculum demanded
it. Yet, studying the sacred art and science of medicine brought
out our differences concerning our origin, purpose, mission,
morals, and value of life. Heated debates on healthcare policy,
abortion, evolution, and religion often followed collaboration
in learning. We quickly fell into two camps, but we remained
kind, helpful, and courteous as we taught each other through
solving medical problems. It took a couple of years, but most of
us learned that all the arguments in the world would not sway
each other's opinions.

My struggle to trust others, along with my suspicion of outsiders, precluded what could have been some great lifelong
friendships. One group of solid Christian guys gelled together
quickly, built each other up, and went on camping trips together.
However, I stayed on the outside looking in, wishing I could be
a part of them. My religious convictions told me they were lost,
but I was the one who felt lost.

During orientation, I sat next to Brennan Dye, a humble, outgoing, great guy. His wife, Sharon, was a liberal COC girl, and so
Sherry and I felt a connection with her. Yet again, though, they

were still outside the CCOC circle. Maybe I could convert them? After all, Brennan was not even a member of the church yet.

Despite my self-righteousness and Brennan's "lost" soul, I learned more about fatherly grace from him than I ever did in church. He had gotten Sharon "in a family way" before marriage. If I'd done something like that and broken the news to my father, I surely would have received judgment and shame. Not so with Brennan's father. He received it as good news, reached out to shake hands, and said, "Congratulations, son, you're going to be a father!" I nearly fell over backward in amazement at such grace, but I decided that somehow, some way, I was going to be a father like that one day.

Brennan and I also clicked with a student named Thomas Carroll right away. Thomas was like a magnet. He was charming, outgoing, funny, and a bit ornery with his occasional cigarette and mixed drink. We'd all sit together in lecture, hang out in the lounge watching ESPN *SportsCenter*, and often have lunch together.

Thomas and I became especially close. He introduced me to Absolute Citron vodka and tonic with a twist of lemon and lime, and he taught me to inhale cigarettes as we celebrated finishing semester exams over a billiards table at Booches. Even though Thomas was a Baptist, he preferred to live a little outside their strict moral code. So did I. Despite the fact that Thomas's wife was Catholic, Sherry and Cathy became like sisters. We were all tight.

Caught in the Give-Up/Try-Hard Cycle

After the first year of med school, Sherry and I moved to Clark, a small town only minutes away from Columbia. With the help of a student loan to cover the downpayment, we were able to purchase a nine-hundred-square-foot home. As it turned out, our neighbor was the minister of the local country CCOC.

Sherman and Violet became like parents to us, bringing fresh vegetables from their garden, giving us homemade sourdough bread and cinnamon rolls, and loaning us gardening tools. The preaching was strict CCOC, but the neighborly love was free and abundant—with one exception. Sherman showed up one afternoon in our backyard, looking to borrow a tool. Instead, he found Sherry sunbathing on the deck in a bikini. The next Sunday's sermon was on modest dress; Sherry was not pleased.

Sherman was the first person I knew who suffered from mental illness. Our relationship was close enough that when my father developed depression a decade later, he felt safe sharing the truth about why he was sometimes sick and missed Sunday preaching duties. As it turned out, he would have to change medications on occasions when things would get tough for him. The side effects rendered him sleepy and homebound for several days. He managed the disease well but was not out in the open about it with everyone, presumably for fear of judgment. I was grateful for the grace he showed me during a dark time. His vulnerability with me was the first and only I had received in the CCOC.

I loved Sherman and Violet, but Sherman's preaching deepened the scars of my youth and reinforced my conviction that, try as I might, I would never stand without condemnation before a holy God. Or maybe I could, if I just tried harder?

Doubts and fears aside, I invited my med school friends into the Clark CCOC fold. Brennan and Sharon attended with us, along with another med school classmate, Jeff, and his strictly Southern CCOC wife, Maggie. I taught our class on Sunday mornings and used every opportunity, while studying the book of Matthew, to convince them that baptism was absolutely necessary for regeneration by God. My goal was to see Jeff and Brennan get baptized. Jeff finally gave in to our version of the gospel and was immersed for the remission of his sins. I now wonder what role my spiritual abuse and haranguing played in the later demise of his marriage and his conviction that he, too, could never be right with God.

Because the third and fourth years of medical school required frequent on-call shifts, Sherry and I decided to sell our house in Clark for a small profit and move into a duplex in Columbia. That move put us closer to the hospital and reunited us with our college church friends, which led us to spend a great deal of time with our old pals, Darius and Jada. By this time, Darius had become a new partner with the local surgical group. We spent many weekends with them, enjoying conversations about the superiority of an orthopaedic lifestyle over all of the other medical and surgical subspecialties. His mentorship played a big role in my choosing to pursue a career in orthopaedics, and we dreamed that one day we might work together as partners and brothers in Christ.

Within the life of the spiritually abused, there exists a "give-up/try-hard" cycle. Thomas and Cathy caught me during the give-up cycle, where I could relax and enjoy life. However, being back at the Columbia church filled me with dread and shame, which convinced me that it was time to try hard again. Thomas and I enjoyed the occasional social drink, but we never got drunk. Nevertheless, in the try-hard cycle, there are no gray areas.

I began to see Thomas's friendship as a corrupting influence. I nitpicked him and pushed him away, along with my other social drinking classmates. I isolated Sherry and myself from the Carrolls. It was unfair to her, and it hurt us all. Unbeknownst to me, I was destroying something great for the sake of something inside me that I couldn't control, let alone understand. All I knew was that I was headed for hell and had better straighten up. By mistrusting Thomas and Cathy, I gave up what were likely the best friends I've ever had. I loved them and still do. I miss them to this day. Later, I apologized, but I suppose the damage was already done, or maybe that is just the shame talking.

My care of an HIV+ patient admitted to the VA for *pneumocystis carinii* pneumonia demonstrates my neurosis for perfection quite well. He was my first patient on my first rotation, and he had fulminant AIDS at a time when HIV was poorly understood and dreadfully feared. I was tasked with drawing my first arterial blood gas sample. To obtain an accurate result, no air could be left within the syringe. After successfully drawing the blood sample from the patient's radial artery, I tipped the syringe up to push any air out of the column of HIV-infected blood.

When the blood hit the Gore-Tex tip, the syringe was sealed. I saw a little air still in the column. Panicking at the thought of turning in a less-than-perfect sample, I pushed a little too hard. *Pop!* It sounded like gunfire when the Gore-Tex tip shot off the syringe, spraying HIV-infected blood all over the ceiling, the wall, and the back of my short white lab coat. Evidently, I was quick enough upon hearing the sound to bend forward and protect my face, preventing HIV from infecting me through the vulnerability of my eyes, nose, and mouth.

In an effort to protect my reputation, I immediately started to clean up the mess without considering the risks. I couldn't let anyone know that I had failed, that a new sample must be drawn, that I was an idiot. The slight sting of a speck of "dust" in my eye brought me back to reality. I was sure it was blood. I rushed downstairs to see Dr. Eglensen, an infectious disease attending with whom I had been working on an orthopaedic research project.

He was kind and sympathetic, slowly irrigating my eye with a couple of liters of normal saline as I lay on the couch in his office. "The solution to pollution is dilution," or so I desperately hoped. I had to wait three months to be certain that I had not developed antibodies to HIV. Sherry and I had to abstain from sex the whole time, though we might have used condoms toward the end. I swore that I would never again put my wife and future family at risk by working around blood, and there was no way in hell I would ever become a surgeon. Obviously, I broke that vow.

Disappointed and Lonely

The pinnacle of medical school had nothing to do with my career. At the beginning of my fourth year, Sherry and I were blessed with the arrival of our first son, Spencer David Hockman. Having a child of my own changed my view of fatherly love. The feelings I had for Spencer did not align with what I had been taught about how Father God feels toward His children. Spencer brought great joy to my life, and I was certain I could never view him the way God apparently viewed me.

During college and medical school, my earthly dad and I had become much closer because of his consistent support. I used to call home discouraged, and he would respond, "What else would you be doing?" With those and many other wise words, he encouraged me to stay faithful to my dream. Yet, Dad's love for me and my new love for Spencer could not connect the dots and allow me to envision Father God's unconditional love for me. I was still too busy trying hard to earn it.

My graduate school accomplishments should have been a source of pride and reassurance, but I have a keen eye for maximizing the negative. I graduated magna cum laude as a part of the Alpha Omega Alpha Honor Medical Society and matched into my second-choice orthopaedic residency. Magna cum laude is second best to summa cum laude, an honor I had been robbed of as a Missouri undergraduate because I didn't have enough credit hours on the Columbia campus to receive Latin honors or be a part of Phi Beta Kappa. During my junior year, I had wanted to be among the first inductees into the Alpha Omega Alpha honor society, but I didn't make it until my senior year. Before match day, I had switched my top two residency choices between Wichita, Kansas, and Greenville, South Carolina, numerous times. I finally decided to make South Carolina my number one, only to be matched to Wichita. Both were great programs, but I still felt second best, not good enough. That theme continued at graduation when I felt especially lonely, not having my good friends Thomas and Cathy to celebrate with.

Chapter 12

HOPE KNOCKS ON THE DOOR DURING RESIDENCY

Mother

She baked my favorite cookies
    And thinks I do not taste
More than just the sweetness
    But of the pain erased.

She kisses my feverish cheek
    And thinks I do not feel
The tender touch of grace
    That has the power to heal.

She cleaned the whole house today
    And thinks I do not smell
The fragrance of her work
    That helps to keep us well.

She spoke to my teacher last night
    And thinks I did not hear
They talked of my behavior
    And how to calm my fear.

She taps my daddy under the table sometimes
    And thinks I do not see
She is trying to guide him
    To be more gentle with me.

She is my amazing mother
    And I think she should be praised
For all her amazing love
    She shines on all my days.

MOVING TO WICHITA to start my orthopaedic surgery residency renewed my pursuit of moral perfection. I hoped to find new friends, a new church, and a new me free of cursing, lusting, and libations, but as it turned out, most of my coresidents were partiers. Their greatest debauchery occurred after the fall and spring visiting professorships when they treated themselves to a night at the strip clubs. Ben Rempel and I were among the few exceptions who did not participate. Ben was a devout Mennonite teetotaler. My goal was to be like him: above it all.

One night, Ben and I were on call together, and we began discussing spiritual matters. I wasn't sure of his goal (or if he had one), but my mission was crystal clear. I intended to proselytize this wayward believer and bring him into the CCOC. When our discussion of baptism turned to Romans 6, where the apostle Paul likens baptism to the death, burial, and resurrection of Christ, I thought I was ready to knock it out of the park and prove to

Ben that water immersion was indeed necessary for salvation. However, Ben's simple response was that the image of Romans 6 was a daily event in his life. He said he was constantly seeking to "die to self," being immersed in God's grace and raised up in Christ. He looked to grace alone through faith alone in Christ alone. However, I was focused on myself, my doctrine, and my proof texts.

After an hour of gentle debate, Ben asked, "David, when you die, do you know where you will go?" It was two in the morning, and we were still standing outside our separate call rooms.

"I'd like to think I'd go to heaven," I responded.

"You would like to think that?" he questioned in a slow, deliberate manner.

"Yeah, if I've prayed for forgiveness and repented before I died, I think He will likely take me to heaven," I stated sheepishly, with my eyes staring at the ground.

"David, the difference between you and me is that I know where I'm going," he said, and with that, he opened the door to his call room and left me with my thoughts.

As I entered my own room, tears streamed down my face. I stayed up for another hour, praying to God in anger, wondering why I couldn't have the assurance that Ben had. I wept bitterly, the kind of crying that fills a dozen tissues with snot and tears and makes you feel like you've had a head cold for days. I was as confused as I was congested. Why couldn't I have Ben's confidence in God to save me? How could I keep trying and never measure up?

As if that were not depressing enough, residency was filled with death. Early on, during my pulmonary medicine rotation in my internship year, we had three or four deaths every week. When we weren't adjusting ventilators, we were pulling the plugs.

Perhaps the saddest moment during my internship came when a little girl died on my pediatric intensive care rotation. That night, I came home angry and took my emotions out on my family, losing my temper and yelling, only to break down crying later and apologize.

The nights on trauma call brought more misery. We served two level-one trauma centers, and on some nights when we were especially busy, the sadness would overwhelm me. I was too sensitive to watch women and children die. I could barely take it at times. Every time I finished my work in the trauma bay, I would spend ten to fifteen minutes crying in the restroom, releasing as much of the grief as possible. After I felt my face was no longer red or my eyes swollen, I would go back out, "once more into the fray."

Here's a typical day, as described in an essay I wrote at that time:

The Five-Year-Old Girl

Mother's Day morning brought a surprise: a new admission. I had set the alarm to give me only enough time to make rounds and get ready for church. Needless to say, the phone call home to my three-week postpartum wife to tell her I would not be home in time to attend church with her and our two sons on Mother's Day was not an easy one. Her disappointment, which was masked by a dutiful and graceful display of understanding, was bittersweet.

As the orthopaedic surgery intern on the pulmonary medicine service, I felt somewhat out of place. The two fields are at opposite ends of the spectrum of patient care. I signed up to deal with relatively healthy patients, make their quality of life better through surgery, and avoid the emotions of interacting with dying patients. Pulmonary medicine involves the most critically ill, dying patients on ventilators. Specialists in this field face death nearly every day, making decisions along with the patients and their families that may either hasten or prolong the end of life. Clearly, admitting a dying patient on Mother's Day is not a part of the career I had envisioned.

Mrs. M was a rheumatoid patient who had numerous recent admissions for various skin and orthopaedic problems. She presented with aspiration pneumonia secondary to her narrowed esophagus, which had been dilated many times. All the classic signs of the most advanced rheumatoid disease were present in her. Perhaps what made her seem so frail was the steroid-induced atrophy of her skin. The gentlest touch to bond with Mrs. M could easily result in the tearing of her skin.

While in the emergency room, quickly poring over the chart before I went to examine Mrs. M, I heard a large man (Mrs. M's son) scream at a nurse that he wanted to see the charge nurse immediately. Five days before admission, the family had walked out of the hospital with the patient after determining that her care was inadequate. In an effort to help protect Mrs. M's skin, they were adamant that no one wear jewelry when working with her. My first impression of the family was that they would not be satisfied with anything we did.

I could not have been more wrong.

Walking on eggshells, I approached Mrs. M's room. The concern and pain were evident in everyone in the room, especially the patient. She barely had enough strength to complain, but her ten-inch-thick chart of admissions over the last five years showed only the surface of her suffering. Mr. M assured us that his wife wanted no heroic measures, so we proceeded within our limits to do everything possible for (or more appropriately, to) Mrs. M.

Due to her recent MRSA cellulitis, we felt Vancomycin was indicated. The problem was that she needed a central line. The attending consulted the general surgery resident to place the line so the attending could go home to be with his mother for Mother's Day. Since it was already past time for my congregation's worship services to begin, I decided to stay and place the line under general surgery supervision. I had only a few prior experiences in line placement, and I wanted the practice. Regretfully, after two internal jugular attempts, holding pressure for five minutes on a bleeding carotid, and finally a subclavian attempt, we finally had access. The catlike cries throughout the procedure made for a melancholy Mother's Day. The general surgery resident's reaction was that some lines go easy, and some don't. Hers didn't.

The next morning, I determined that Mrs. M was septic and had developed a severe metabolic acidosis. The bicarbonate temporized her condition, but in the face of an overwhelming infection in a severely debilitated patient, I wondered if any further treatment was warranted. I had already made her suffer through my central line placement. Was I now going to continue with therapy, which I knew was only prolonging the inevitable? Was I going to lengthen her suffering? What is an orthopaedic intern doing in this critical medical situation?

Early that morning, I spoke with Mr. M about his wife's rapidly deteriorating condition and questioned how he would like to proceed. Unfortunately, I also had to inform him of a change in attendings. The doctor they met on Mother's Day was a kind, compassionate man with excellent patient skills. Their new attending physician, while adequate, was the lesser of the two. I remained as the constant face in the process and agreed to arrange a meeting with the family, the new attending, and me.

As I walked to the elevator, I saw one of the patient's daughters and stopped to inform her of the meeting and to listen to any concerns she had. We talked briefly, but before I left, she told me that I had no idea how many doctors would have avoided her and kept on going. She said she was thankful to have me as her mother's physician. Is this what I was trying to avoid by deciding on a career in orthopaedics?

A calm discussion took place in a room eight feet by eight feet, with ten chairs and fourteen people. The family said that Mrs. M would not want any further treatment, only comfort care. I reflected on my narrow-minded days as a first-year medical student, shocked and appalled at the idea of withholding treatment to a dying patient. My ignorance was bliss. As a five-year-old girl sat in the middle of the room coloring in her coloring book, I wanted to be as detached from the situation as she was. I wanted my innocence back. Her world was so perfect—even her coloring book was designed so that she needed only to scribble with the same pen, and yet all the colors magically appeared in their proper place, producing a wonderful picture of Donald Duck and his family.

After the attending stated that removing Mrs. M's oxygen would likely bring her death within one to twenty minutes, tears filled everyone's eyes except the attending and the five-year-old girl. An extra effort was made to ensure we understood exactly what the patient wanted, and then the attending and I left, but not before we were showered with praise and thanks for our perfect handling of Mrs. M's care.

Following this highly emotional meeting with the family, the first four words from my attending to me were "From a medico-legal standpoint . . . ." I suppose his complete lack of emotional attachment is a good example of how to deal with constant death and dying. However, I doubted I could ever deny myself the privilege of feelings.

Approaching Mrs. M after the meeting was quite difficult. A lump rose in my throat, and tears filled my eyes as I made her aware that removing all treatment except pain control would quickly hasten her death. I asked her if that was what she wanted, and she nodded yes. The entire family was in the room, crying over the impending death. Immediately after attempting to comfort the patient, the family, and myself by telling them I'd pray for Mrs. M, I was embarrassed to see my attending had just entered the room. Ashamed, I wondered whether I was embarrassed by my inability to do anything for the patient or by having mentioned praying in front of my attending. Feeling woefully inadequate but justified in my management of the patient, I left the room, met with continued gratitude and the open arms of several family members.

Watching the monitor outside the patient's room, I waited for death. My attending left me to pronounce the patient. I collected the chart and started to write a pronouncement note even before the patient had died, but I stopped myself. Was I this god-like that I was bringing death within the next few hours? Or was I trying to be efficient and hurry home to escape? I walked in to check on Mrs. M once, and she appeared comfortable and denied feeling any pain. Then, twenty minutes after the oxygen was stopped, the family invited me into the room. Strangely, I felt hopeful as I entered the room. Mrs. M was dead.

I am amazed at the gratitude the family expressed in our handling of Mrs. M's last hospitalization. They were so affectionate toward me that at times I felt uncomfortable. One daughter said she could tell I understood more about the level of suffering her mother and family had endured than any other doctor in the last five years. I have never felt so much pain and, at the same time, received so much reward. At one point near the end of the day, I even wondered if I had missed my calling.

But after going home, gaining some distance, and being short-tempered with my family, I realized that complete detachment is really the only way I could cope with death and dying. I want to pour my emotions into my family, not drain them at work until there is none left for my loved ones. So, I chose orthopaedics. I choose to be like that five-year-old girl.

Porn, Booze, and Shame

Sundays brought a welcome reprieve. Our new CCOC was considered a bit on the left end of the CCOC spectrum due to its stance on grace. I didn't discover that stance until I'd attended for a couple of years. They seemed pretty hardline on doctrine, but they were led by two gentle men, Phillip and Barry. They both had great kids and treated us like we had been attending there for decades. We grew close to them, and I hoped to one day become an elder just like them.

The only evident downside of the church was the lack of people our age. Having no couples our age, we contented ourselves in cultivating our relationships with Phil and Barry's families. They inspired me to press on in the faith, and I needed all the help I could get, struggling as I was with the shame of hidden sin in my life.

One night on call, I discovered that the call rooms had a supply of *Penthouse* and *Hustler* magazines. My libido hadn't changed much since I was a teenager, and so there was a battle before me. The pressure of residency was intense, only surpassed by the pressure I put on myself to be perfect. So, I failed and looked. Then, on the next call that evening, I wouldn't look. Then, I would fail again and throw them away. When another stash showed up, I would either throw them away or look first and then throw them away. I didn't get it. Why did this tempt me? What was wrong with me? I thought God must despise me. Full of shame, I told no one.

Even worse, during my five years of residency, this new thing called the internet began to supply pornography to any available computer terminal at any time of the day or night, free of cost. What an evil game-changer in my battle for self-control! Thank God there was only super slow dial-up at the time.

For the first time in my life, at age thirty, I discussed the temptation to lust with my junior resident, Hal, who was a devout Christian. By the time I met him, I was less interested in proselytizing and more interested in learning. Ben had helped me realize that there was plenty I did not know. Hal and I had grown pretty close through conversations on God, faith, and grace. When the topic of pornography came up, he directed me to a book by Stephen Arterburn and Fred Stoeker entitled *Every Man's Battle*. The first thing I did after purchasing it was to hide it from Sherry.

The next Saturday, I was on call, stuck all day and night at the hospital with no responsibility unless the pager went off. The pager never went off, and I was able to read *Every Man's Battle* from cover to cover. It was the first book I ever read in a single day. My eyes were opened to the fact that I was not alone in the struggle for sexual purity. The stories in the book sounded a lot like my own stories. Men are wired to lust, but God created that need to be fulfilled within marriage, not pornography.

After dog-earing and marking up the pages, I came up with a plan. However, one thing was for sure: I was not going to complete the last step described in the book. The book quotes James and reminds the reader that true healing can only come through confession and accountability, but there was no way I would ever let anyone know about my secret shame. Confession would be strictly between God and me. I would win the battle by my own effort, following the book's techniques for avoiding lustful temptations. The term for this approach is "sin management," and it never works.

I was proud that I'd never gone to the strip clubs with my fellow residents, though I did go secretly by myself for about five minutes once. I felt too dirty to stay in that environment. I hated my duplicitous, shameful self for occasionally turning to pornography in private. I desperately want to be morally upstanding. To me, that is what it meant to be a Christian.

At the same time, some areas of morality were unclear to me. I still couldn't decide if drinking alcohol in moderation was sinful or not. The CCOC left no room for opinion, but I liked alcohol, and Jesus turned water to wine—good wine, in fact. I decided to follow Jesus's lead and ignore the CCOC.

Drinking with my fellow residents was just part of being in community with them. There was alcohol in the homes of each of my three classmates. The visiting professor programs, receptions, golf tournament, and every single social function all served in abundance. Plus, I loved beer, vodka tonics, and gin and tonics. I was tired of trying so hard all the time to avoid it.

I decided that my only remaining battle for morality was giving up lust. Out of a deep love for Sherry and a desire not to betray her with my eyes, I fought hard against lustful temptation. It was my ongoing private struggle. I would never give up the fight, but I would drink. To my dismay, I still felt ashamed about both.

Heavenbound?

Shaken up by my conversation with Ben and my inability to be morally perfect, I finally had a conversation with Philip, one of the elders, about salvation. I'd known him long enough now that I felt safe with him, so I asked him about my conversation with Ben. It just didn't make sense to me that the Bible was filled with so many promises on the surety of salvation, yet we were convinced not to trust them. His reply was a gift of grace. He told me that we are not like yo-yos, pulled in and out of grace. Philip was convinced, contrary to CCOC oral tradition, that a Christian could sin and still go to heaven without praying and repenting first. It sounded so liberal, but it felt true.

Phillip talked with me about how God sees the heart in spite of the behavior. He believed that a Christian could so repetitively sin as to walk away from God but that one sin did not represent such a change of heart. According to my understanding of the conversation with Phillip, my salvation was more secure than I had thought, but it was still not completely certain. However, I was pleased to learn that my name was not repeatedly written, erased, and rewritten in the Lamb's Book of Life. Still I wondered, could I trust him?

Sherry's twin sister married a Baptist college graduate named Lonnie, and one Christmas, I had an enlightening conversation with him about the necessity of baptism in order to receive salvation. It got a bit heated, with Scriptures being hurled back and forth. What really startled me, though, was the way the conversation ended. I had been taught that the CCOC was being safe because of all the restrictions and requirements, but Lonnie pointed out that we were not safe at all. In fact, he pointed out that if we were trying to be saved by works like baptism, then we may not be saved at all. Good God! Was it possible I wasn't even saved at my baptism?

These spiritual discussions were driving me mad, or more likely, revealing my madness.

My coresidents and I also had our fair share of religious discussions. We grew as close as I would allow, not fully trusting them. Mark was the son of an attending who was more interested in musicology than in theology. Andrew was a devout Catholic, and our discussion on authority drove me insane. He valued Scripture and tradition equally, while I proudly claimed to follow only Scripture, but in truth, I clung to Scripture and the CCOC oral tradition. I was not able to grasp that similarity at the time. Now I see that they are pretty much the same. Perhaps that is why our conversations drove me mad. Andrew and I had a better time when we stuck with conversations about Budweiser, orthopaedics, and family.

Rod became a close friend when he went through some tough times after his wife committed adultery. Though I was sure to heap on him an unhealthy dose of CCOC dogma about marriage, divorce, and remarriage, mostly I just listened and tried to be supportive. I have been terrible at keeping in touch with my old friends, but I love those guys like brothers.

A Better Father

Despite all the religious ramblings ruminating in my mind, I managed to stay fairly upbeat and happy. Residency was like family. Our coordinator, Carlita, was a Christian single mom who treated us like her own kids. The chairman was like a wise grandfather whose sayings would often come to mind when I was operating. Most of the residents had spouses and kids, and the "ortho wives" would get together for playdates with their kids. It was a supportive yet eclectic group.

Our family grew by two during residency. Alex, our youngest son, was born near the end of my internship. Then at our "halfway" party, Sherry and I dressed up as Gilligan and the Skipper, only Sherry was the Skipper because of her pregnant belly. Paige, our long-awaited daughter, arrived a few months later. Andrew's kids were about the same ages as ours, so we all had a ton of fun together when we weren't studying and working like slaves at the hospital.

Perhaps equally important to the growth of knowledge and expertise in orthopaedics was the tangential angle my spiritual path had taken during residency. No doubt, I was still deep in CCOC bondage, but I was beginning to think a little differently. I was curious about grace and where it fit into my life. The gospel of grace was as attractive as it was elusive, but I could not let go of the new truth that grace could cover sin without following a formula for forgiveness.

I saw how pathetic my spiritual path was. My inconsistencies were not lost on me. Shame was always in my field of view, but at the end of residency, I had three children to lead. Would they become a spiritual wreck like me, or would I find a better way? I was on a mission to learn. Barry, the other elder, had taught me one secret about fatherhood: keep the kids talking by sharing your life with them. I hoped that after enough tangential realignments, I might just find the truth and become a good father and spiritual leader.

Chapter 13

FELLOWSHIP IN DC

Haven

The happiness I know in loving you is only the beginning
Of the joy I encounter each day as I watch you nurture our children.
I love the smile on your face when they say something unexpected,
The sound of your voice as you introduce each of them to me on the phone,
The kind way you teach them how to say "please" and "thank you" and "I love you,"
The look in your eyes when you point to Paige as she skips and runs,
The hushed tone in your voice when you ask me to watch Spencer and Alex giggle,
The joy you express while playing with them,
The small lap that somehow holds all three of them,
The patient waiting while they help you cook or clean,
The gentle embrace to sooth hurt feelings or skinned knees,

The anger at a stranger's indignation over their rare episodes of
public misbehavior,
The godly voice of correction and instruction,
The impartial way you mediate between them,
The example of godliness you set before them.
You make our home a haven.

WITH RESIDENCY IN the rearview mirror,
my family and I were off to Washington, DC, for
a one-year fellowship in adult reconstruction. The
temptation to go to Phoenix and put in equal hours on the golf
course as in the operating room was strong, but Darius encouraged
me to accept an invitation to one of the best hip and knee fellow-
ships in the world, alongside some of the field's great innovators.
Our plan was coming together, and I had a spot at the Columbia
Orthopaedic Group waiting for me when I returned.

I also took Darius's advice on attending the Andan Meadow
Church of Christ in Maryland. The preacher at Andan Meadow
was quite a character. We enjoyed our time there, where we
were treated like family. We got to know plenty of other young
families. They came from all over the country and had jobs I
never knew existed, like cartographers and geologists. Many of
us were only at Andan Meadow for a brief time, but that didn't
stop the local members from taking us in.

One family was particularly inspiring yet simultaneously
depressing. This middle-aged Caucasian couple raised their two
biological kids into adulthood and then adopted a sibling set of
four black boys, whom they loved as their own. They seemed like
great parents, and, of course, the family deserved high praise.
Why did I say depressing? Because these four adopted boys
who had never known anything about CCOC were now fully
immersed in it and all its many extrabiblical demands.

The oldest son was a superstar baseball player, bound for the high school state championship. But he skipped a playoff game because it was on a Wednesday night, and he would not miss Bible study. He was spoken of in the local newspaper as a modern Eric Liddell, but I didn't quite see it that way. All of the childish regrets I'd felt about missing *Diff'rent Strokes* on Wednesday nights and *Walt Disney World* on Sunday nights had hardened into a mature disdain for the legalistic demands of gaining grace. I was beginning to see that the CCOC rules were not only not working in my own life but were causing harm in the lives of others.

Josh McDowell rightly stated that rules without relationship lead to rebellion. My favorite sins did not find repentance in rules, but "relationship with Jesus" wasn't something I understood as part of my spirituality at the time. If that adopted young man had been my son, I would have encouraged him to keep his commitment to the baseball team and not be so hard on himself for missing a Wednesday night Bible study. That's quite a change from my past when I would have been first in line to cheer him on for standing up for the "truth." My moralistic, spiritually abused heart longed for freedom, but I lacked the courage to find a new direction. So I stuck with what I knew and continued searching for elusive grace and peace, blindly groping in the darkness of the CCOC.

Change, Change, Change

The year of surgical training was both challenging and rewarding. Performing hip and knee replacements came naturally to me. After a lifetime of hoping for something I could be good at, I had finally found it. In residency, I had always been handed the knife early in each rotation because of my reputation as a good surgeon, and fellowship was no different. I had found what God created me to do.

Unfortunately, this calm assurance was quickly interrupted by chaos when Sherry's parents called from Missouri to announce that they were divorcing after thirty-eight years of marriage. With two-, four-, and six-year-olds watching her every move, Sherry swallowed her feelings and put on a happy face for our children. However, behind closed doors, she was devastated. Maybe being 1,000 miles away helped her cope with the upcoming life change. More than the distance, her faith and mental toughness carried her through the year with poise.

In October, we flew back to Columbia to buy a home and meet Mason Lowler, an orthopaedic sales rep who assisted Darius. He seemed eager to befriend us. My account represented about $2 million to $3 million in sales, so I'm sure he was motivated at least partly by the potential commission. We stayed at his house that weekend, even though I'd never even met him before that. Our wives hit it off terrifically. On Sunday, we attended Northside together with Darius and his family, who had been successful in proselytizing Mason to the CCOC.

While in Columbia, I also had the opportunity to interview candidates to be my assistant in clinic and surgery. The first candidate was a man with hair longer than my wife's. He didn't seem like a go-getter and wasn't a good fit. The next candidate was a physician assistant fresh out of school, but she seemed way too gung-ho. Last, I interviewed Joy Blu, a newly graduated nurse practitioner with ten years of nursing experience on the orthopaedic floor. She had more ortho experience than I did. Our personalities matched perfectly, and I admired her reputation as the best nurse on the floor.

When I returned to DC, I reported back to the operating room (OR) crew. I told them I'd found the perfect person to be my first assistant. The only problem was that she was attractive. I had always planned to hire a man since I knew I'd be working closely with my assistant all day, every day. A man posed no temptation. What if I wasn't strong enough? What if people talked?

I agonized over the decision until Elizabeth, a scrub tech for over thirty years, set me straight. In her slow Southern drawl, she said, "Now, David, what if that was little Paige. Would you want some man not to hire her because she's a girl?" I loved Elizabeth, and her opinion made it clear that I shouldn't act out of fear, especially since my wife didn't object to hiring a female assistant. So Joy got the job.

Betrayal at Home

As the year drew to a close, I had an opportunity to stay on as a junior attending. This opportunity would have led to fame within the orthopaedic community. I would get to publish multiple research papers, travel the globe, give lectures, and operate on the elite who came to the clinic. My ego said yes, but my heart said no. My father had often warned my brother and me against too much travel. DC was all about power and money. I couldn't bear the thought of raising my family in that environment. I knew I was better off in Columbia with Darius as a partner, Northside as my church, Mason as my sales rep and new best friend, and Joy as my assistant.

Mason loved to serve others, which is a great strength in ortho sales. The more he helped to get my practice established, the sooner he could earn commission, but I sensed that he truly cared for me. Mason helped to set up everything I needed in the OR, which was a huge deal to me. We went to the American Club together for a wine-and-dine golf conference in Kohler,

Wisconsin, where I learned to enjoy cabernet and several new techniques in pain management and "minimally invasive" surgery. I was ready to get started in Columbia and take on the world, but Mason had some bad news for me.

I thought I would be working side by side with my perfect Christian friend, Darius. He was known for missing Wednesday night partnership meetings to attend church, never cussing in the OR, holding Bible studies with work associates, teaching Sunday school, leading worship, housing visiting preachers for week-long revivals, never drinking alcohol, and having four perfect kids. An icon within the CCOC and a perfect moral specimen, Darius was having an adulterous affair with his married nurse.

Honestly, the news devastated me. My mentor was defiantly living in sin while still attending church with his family three times a week. His wife knew about it. The partners knew about it. The whole hospital knew. He had shut himself off from his partners and me. I actually got a call from a senior partner, who insisted on meeting me for dinner just to discuss with me whether or not I was going to turn out like Darius, withdrawn and aloof. I tried to reassure him, but I kept thinking of 1 Corinthians 10:12, which says to let anyone who thinks that he stands take heed lest he fall. If Satan's attack could fell Darius, what about me? I had some serious soul searching to do.

Before returning to Columbia, I finally got a phone call through to Darius. I wish I hadn't. He informed me that he didn't think there was enough work for me as a hip and knee surgeon and that I would essentially be competing with him within the group. It was clear he didn't want me there, but my family and I were anxious to start a new life close to our hometowns. The Columbia Orthopaedic Group's reputation would be enough to ensure my initial success. No matter what, though, I was ready to compete. Game on.

Chapter 14

Unwelcome Return to Darkness

My Wife and God

Time and circumstance reduced me to melancholy,
Yet you remained hopeful.

I withdrew in isolation,
While your arms stayed open.

Despite my volatile temperament,
You were a calming presence.

The walls were closing in,
Your strength held me safely.

Drowning in despair,
You gave me hope.

Through vision blurred with tears,
I could always see your joy.

Though the darkness hovers as an ominous cloud,
The light of your presence lingers faithfully.

You illuminate the path to happiness,
You shine forth a new optimism,

You brighten my fallen countenance,
And I will have joy.

SANS ONE, MY partners were all supportive in referring patients to me, and during my first full year in practice, I performed 250 joint replacements. In my first full calendar year, 2004, I performed 329. Joy and I proved to be a great team, and we developed a reputation for having a kind, patient bedside manner. There was plenty of work to do, and I was off to a great start. Surprisingly, Darius even allowed Joy to scrub in with him to learn how to be a good assistant. It looked as though God was working all things together for good. I was right there with Him, working hard to prove myself worthy of His favor.

Even so, feeling like I had something to prove didn't serve me well on my first case as a newly trained surgeon. It was my first case without anyone looking over my shoulder, so I knew it had to be perfect. The patient was an eighty-five-year-old with a broken hip. I skillfully performed a partial hip replacement and asked Joy to pop the hip back in place. As we assessed the patient's hip, we heard a crack, and the thigh rotated ninety degrees in a direction it wasn't meant to.

"What was that?" Joy asked.

"Her femur just broke. How hard were you rotating?" I replied softly.

"Not hard at all. What are we going to do now?"

"Fix it."

What a disaster for a surgeon's first case! When I explained to the patient's family what had transpired in the OR, they nodded with familiarity and informed me that she had been having a lot of stress fractures lately. Even though I had taken what I thought was a thorough history, they evidently hadn't seen a need to include that little tidbit. If I'd known about the history of stress fractures going into it, I would have changed my surgical plan. It taught me that patients and their families are unreliable historians. Thankfully, the patient healed and seemed to do well for a while. However, the poor lady died about a year later from metastatic pancreatic cancer.

The strangest thing about that case was the way others reacted to it. No one else seemed concerned about the complication. The partners still had confidence in me. Still, I couldn't stop mentally flogging myself for months, and I made sure everyone knew how upset I was with having a complication. I wanted to make sure everyone knew just how deeply I cared and how much I strove for perfection. Little did I know that my overreaction was completely natural for someone who had suffered spiritual abuse and had developed a shame-based identity. I was insecure and ashamed of myself, and I didn't even realize it.

The Beginning of the End

Returning to Northside seemed like a homecoming. Many of the old families were still members, and I reunited with many of my old college buddies who had stayed in Columbia. The only difference was that Darius and his family were aloof toward me because of the turmoil in their home, and I found it impossible to reconnect with them. Most of the church seemed clueless about what was going on with Darius, but I wasn't about to gossip.

Eventually, all the elders knew about Darius's affair but did not seem to hold him accountable. Darius showed no signs of repentance. I would watch him "close talk" and flirt with his nurse Wednesday in the OR and lead singing at church that same night. Self-righteously, I couldn't stand the hypocrisy and wanted justice–only for him, not me. I had my own hidden sin. Jada and the kids were hurting, and the church seemed to be doing nothing about it.

His fall from grace was apparent to everyone outside the church, and too many people delighted in his moral decline. His behavior positively impacted my new practice, as I got a lot of referrals from doctors who no longer wanted Darius seeing their patients. I felt conflicted. I was trying to be friends with Darius while also taking as many of his referrals as I could. It was awkward to say the least. Nevertheless, Darius rebuffed any attempt by me at "being there" for him, and over time, I came to despise him.

I hated the way the church allowed him to behave. The CCOC believes strictly in church discipline, and I believed Darius should have been disciplined. The elders did nothing. I wondered if maybe they feared a decline in the Sunday offering. Perhaps that explains my bad attitude throughout the whole ordeal. Whatever the case, the lack of response by church leadership was just more of what I had already experienced as a child growing up in the CCOC, namely, a lack of respect for women as equals. My eyes opened to the misogyny within the CCOC, and I began to speak out against it, only to eventually be silenced.

My relationship with Darius remained tumultuous. Neither of us loved the other properly. When one was ready to reconcile, the other remained unrepentant. One Wednesday night, Darius walked forward at church and confessed his sin. I reached out to help in various ways, even offering the same book that helped me, *Every Man's Battle*. Within a year, though, a flirtatious nurse proved to be too much temptation for him.

Jada's sense of rejection was hard to witness. Sherry and I grieved with her. I wanted to stick up for her and all the CCOC women. However, the more I commented in Sunday school about what I saw as the Bible's teaching on equality between women and men, the more the church's leadership seemed to turn against me. I'm sure I could have handled the whole situation better.

To my surprise, in the spring of my second year in Columbia, I was asked to preach a sermon. The preacher was going to be absent one Sunday in October, and they wanted me to fill in. That gave me plenty of time to prepare. My father had taught me to study the Bible using commentaries, Bible dictionaries, and concordances. Those tender moments with him are the ones I cherish. He taught Dan and me to preach, teach, lead singing, serve communion, and pray publicly, all works every good CCOC man was expected to do. Since it seemed the church was becoming divided over several issues (including Darius), I decided to preach on the church as a family, using the acronym FAMILY (forgiveness, accountability, mentoring, inclusivity, love, and you).

Zeal Without Knowledge?

Spiritually, my life was rocky, but my career was going better than expected. My hypercritical, perfectionist eye allowed me to see in increments of millimeters and degrees, a great gift for a bone carpenter. The money was great, and patients' results were even greater. After making partner, I had even greater income potential. My marriage and family were all right on track. I had every reason to be happy, but a nagging sense of spiritual discontentment weighed me down.

I was making more money in a month than my father and mother made all year. Spiritually, it didn't feel right. I felt guilty. Surely God didn't want me and my family to enjoy that money. I wrestled with how much to give back. The CCOC says that tithing is an Old Testament practice, but if the Israelites had to give 10 percent, then under the better covenant of Christ, we should give more. So was that more than 10 percent of pretax or post-tax income? I didn't exactly trust Northside with that much money. Could I give to a missionary instead? Did that count toward my greater than 10 percent?

I didn't know what to do with all that money except to save as much as possible, spend some, and give until it hurt, at least a little. Whether out of guilt or generosity, we gave some to CCOC missionaries in Italy, South Africa, and Zimbabwe, and of course to Northside.

We even had an Italian preacher stay at our home for six weeks after arranging for him to have an ankle surgery here, a surgery he could not afford back home. It felt good to be involved in the church's work in the world, yet my obsession with doing the right thing to gain God's favor was wearing me down.

I saw this obsession so clearly on display in Northside's continued striving for the perfect worship performance. Darnell Williamson was now an elder at Northside, and he worked with a group of songwriters who put together a new hymnal with a supplement full of their new songs, which seemed self-serving to me. We had seminars, classes, practice sessions, all to learn how to "wow" visitors with our deep, meaningful lyrics and perfect four-part harmony. We'd sing in a minor key to show our reverence, in forte to show joy, in pianissimo to show contemplation. If you didn't respond correctly to the song leader's timing, he might stop worship, chastise the crowd, and start over. It was as bizarre as it was controlling. At least, that's how I saw it in my highly critical, judgmental mind.

I once asked Darnell about singing more contemporary songs. I had been listening to Casting Crowns' "Lifesong," MercyMe's "Coming Up to Breathe," and other songs on Christian radio. They spoke grace and truth to me, as I yearned for more out of life. On one occasion, Joy was sitting in my office after our first year in practice, and she looked at me and said, "Is this it? Is this what we worked for? And now we just do it over and over?" My response was a dazed look and a nod, but inwardly, I knew there must be more. The songs from Casting Crowns and MercyMe beckoned me to come closer to God and take a look. I wanted to worship with songs like that, but Darnell misapplied Romans 10:2 and told me I had "zeal but not according to knowledge."

An Ailing Father and an Angel

Back home in Oak Grove, life was not going much better than in Columbia. In fact, they were far worse. Mom got a buyout from AT&T with lifetime good health insurance. She and Dad were set for a great retirement. They just had to sell the store and then start enjoying their golden years. We knew Dad had experienced some recent depression or some sort of change that had affected his confidence, but we could never have imagined what lay ahead.

Unbeknownst to us, Dad was in the early stages of Lewy body dementia. After he began having trouble counting change at the hardware store, Dad and Mom decided to sell the business. Unfortunately, no one was interested in buying. They were forced to liquidate, and on that last day, when everything was 90 percent off, I watched my Dad mentally break down in disgust that his last three decades of labor lay in ruins. That was June 2005. In July, I was traveling back and forth between Columbia and Kansas City to accompany my mom to my dad's doctor's appointments, desperately trying to figure out what was wrong with him. Despite months of investigation by several specialists in neurology and psychiatry, we never got a good answer or a clear diagnosis.

At about that time, Larry Justice appeared in my life to encourage me. I didn't know him, but he showed up one Sunday evening at church, looking unkempt and wearing tattered clothing. I had left my pew to use the restroom when he had entered the sanctuary. At first, he was about to sit in my seat, but then, without seeing me right behind him, he moved up a row. I thought it was odd, but I ignored it. After the service, I tried to make him feel welcome. Others did the same, but he hung around until he could talk to me alone.

He looked me in the eye and told me God wanted him to encourage me to stay true to my family. He then related a story about his family and implored me never to give up, no matter what. He explained he was traveling to Alabama, and I offered to help financially, but he refused. He stated that he only came to deliver that message.

The next day, Sherry saw him at the gas station by our house, trying to sell an old electric jigsaw to raise money. He did need help, so Sherry and I decided to give him twenty dollars for the saw. I have that saw to this day. I'll never get rid of it because it reminds me that when I was seeking justice, God found me and encouraged me to give grace, no matter what. At the time, I thought his warning was completely unnecessary. Little did I know that seven or eight years later, my own marriage would be in trouble. Obviously, God knew I needed the encouragement. My mom told me that she thought Larry was an angel, which is a bizarre thing for a CCOC person to suggest, but I agreed with her.

The encouragement was timely, as my dad's health was quickly deteriorating, and we still had no answers. We finally got a brain MRI, and that's when the doctor broke my mother's heart and told her that Dad was in the beginning stages of Alzheimer's disease. He warned her that depression usually accompanies the early stage. They didn't believe him. Convinced otherwise, they went home and began practicing the Mini-Mental State Exam, which involved tasks such as counting backward by seven, drawing a clock face, and recalling a specific spoken word after other sentences were recited.

The neurologist referred Dad to a psychiatrist and a neuro-cognitive specialist. The psychiatrist confirmed the diagnosis of depression and prescribed Lexapro, which seemed to help. Whether by practice or better cognition, Dad's mini-mental state seemed to get slightly better. The new neurologist was convinced that he had dementia with Parkinsonism, which is really a "wastebasket" term for people who don't meet the full criteria of Parkinson's disease.

Am I Clinically Depressed?

In 2006, I decided to change from one implant company to another. I was unhappy with some aspects of hip and knee implants and thought I had found better implants and instrumentation with the other company. Mason decided to switch companies as well and honor his noncompete clause by working in Kansas City while still living in Columbia. John Lloyd would be my new rep in Columbia. I thought I was a free man in a free country, but the distributors of each company dragged me into a lawsuit because of the change.

For months, I was kept in fear by my lawyer that I could be accused of collusion, which thankfully never came to fruition. This stressor, along with my dad's illness and my issues with Darius and the church, was taking a toll on me mentally. My mother sent me an email in the summer of 2006 expressing her concern that I was depressed. I appreciated her concern but didn't think much of it until a long car ride to Sikeston.

John Lloyd knew a doctor in Cape Girardeau who needed his knees replaced, and he thought that if I gave a lecture on joint replacements to that medical community, I would get to do that doctor's knees and subsequently all the joints he would later refer to me. John and I didn't know each other well, but an eight-hour round-trip car ride changed that. We were both parents with young children, and as we shared our experiences, we discovered a commonality: We were both volatile. I thought I was alone in being easily angered and irritable, but John let me know he'd felt the same way until he got treated for anxiety.

He informed me that excessive irritability is a sign of depression and anxiety. I had no idea, even though I was a physician. It took great courage for him to open up to me about his taking Wellbutrin for anxiety. He cast aside fear of judgment and shared with me what his family doctor had told him about psychiatric medicine. As he put it, no one faults a person with diabetes for needing insulin, so why should anyone fault someone whose brain does not produce enough serotonin? John humbled himself, took medication to calm his anxiety, and was a better father and husband for it. I knew at that moment that I wanted the same, but I was too afraid to act on it. I wrestled with my thoughts.

Can a surgeon take psychiatric meds? Will I lose my license? Will I lose the perfectionist edge that gives me an eye for detail? Will I become a mediocre surgeon? What does taking these medications say about my faith? Do I need to pray more? Do I just not have enough faith? How can I work harder on my depression, anxiety, and irritability? What if I have a complication and the plaintiff finds out I take a psych med? Will I lose everything I've worked for?

Rejected, Silenced, and Confused

As October rolled around, I was preparing to fill in for the pastor and preach one Sunday. I already had my sermon topic picked out, and I was ready to go. However, after more issues at church, I got a call from the elders, and they informed me that I would not be allowed to preach after all. The call came on Saturday night, after I'd already spent days studying and writing the sermon. I was speechless. How did it get to this point? No amount of reasoning would change their minds. The same elder who had taken me into his home when I was a college student with the stomach flu was now refusing even to allow me a voice in his church. I went from heartbroken to furious to terrified within minutes of hanging up.

Rejected and silenced, I panicked. My thoughts raced.

If the CCOC cast me out and if the CCOC was the "one true church," where could I go? Hell was the obvious answer. If they were wrong, then was my entire spiritual life a lie? If they were right and I was wrong, what did that say about who God is? Could that God ever be pleased? Did He even exist? A crisis ensued. I did not know what to believe and certainly had no idea where to find answers. Maybe Christianity was all a lie. No, I knew that wasn't true, didn't I? Was any of this real?

My dad's health only added to the doubt. He was getting worse, having difficulty walking and experiencing low back and neck pain. I decided early in the year that we should look for other causes of his shuffling gait. The lumbar spine MRI showed severe spinal stenosis, and the cervical spine MRI showed the same but with spinal cord impingement. Well, it was no wonder he couldn't walk well or fasten the buttons on his shirts. He started nonoperative treatment, but his condition continued to deteriorate.

That was the last straw. Clinical depression hit me hard. The previous year, in 2005, I had spent a month of evenings alone in my garage, listening to Coldplay, painting the walls and the floors, installing plastic trim work, and crying. Who would have guessed that anything was wrong? Now, I was barely conversing with my family. I had no energy and only wanted to sleep. I wore a happy mask during the day and played the role of a good surgeon, but the nights were dark.

Withdrawn and aloof, I was at the bottom of a dark sea of hopelessness with no way to reach the surface. Finally, while crying profusely in Dr. Shauder's office, I reached out for help and damned the consequences, whatever they might be. He prescribed Wellbutrin, and within a month, I was feeling quite a bit better, just in time to help care for my dad after his posterior lumbar spinal decompression and fusion.

With a medicated mind, I never missed a beat in the clinic or the OR, but I still had no clarity on God. He seemed so far away, so far from helping. After much rumination and conversation with Sherry and the Lowlers, we all decided to attend the Clark CCOC, thinking that CCOC was still the right way to go. Maybe the Northside group was just a bunch of bad apples.

As long as the Northside church didn't exercise church discipline against us, maybe the Clark group would accept us. It was a gamble for sure, but with freshly treated depression, I dared to give it a try. Thankfully, Northside took no action. If they had disciplined me, I would have been marked as "one who causes discord." The Northside members would then be obligated to shun me until I repented and was restored to fellowship with the Northside congregation. The downstream effect could mean the Clark church might refuse to allow me to join.

Fortunately, Sherman and Violet, my old neighbors from Coleman Street, along with the rest of the congregation at Clark, gave us a warm welcome. Their loving embraces made us feel like family. Not a lot of questions were asked. They were just happy to have us, and we were glad to be there.

Sadly, that feeling didn't last long.

As I sat through a sermon on the formula to regain God's forgiveness for sins committed after your baptism, I had a terrible feeling that I was guilty of misleading my own children. I no longer believed in this legalistic dogma. How could I subject my kids to the same spiritual beatings I had received from the CCOC? Of course, the bigger question was how I could ever leave and be OK with God and my family?

I no longer believed what the CCOC taught. I had been spending late nights browsing websites like theophilus.org and exchurchofchrist.com, and I found a common bond with others who grew up as I did. I was beginning to think that maybe the Holy Spirit does indwell believers and seal them somehow, in some way, at least temporarily. Maybe grace and love do cover a multitude of sins through faith, not works (not that I was ready to give up works).

But what about celebrating Christmas? What about using church funds to support parachurch organizations? What about having fellowship meals in the church building? What about instrumental music in worship? Could I throw away all of these teachings as well? One thing seemed clear to me: If the CCOC was wrong about one doctrine, then all of their legalistic teachings were suspect. Maybe they were wrong about everything. Confusion took up permanent residence in my spiritual life.

Uncle Ray to the Rescue

Wanting to leave the CCOC but unable to, I turned to my uncle Ray for help. I sent him emails with my questions. By this time, Ray had earned a graduate degree in theology. We corresponded for a few weeks with many emails going back and forth. He prayed diligently for me and answered my questions with loving concern. His answers were gentle and based on Scripture. He became a spiritual giant in my life and gradually helped me feel safe about leaving the CCOC.

Music also played a large role in leaving. Casting Crowns, MercyMe, Chris Tomlin, Matt Maher, and others were speaking truth into my life about unconditional love, the Father's affection for His hurting children, and the gift of grace. Most importantly, yet most unfamiliar to me, I learned about freedom in Christ. Certainly, all I had known was bondage. Freedom appealed to me as a proud American, but freedom in Christ never made sense to me. Serving from love rather than fear made sense, but I didn't know how to serve that way. God's love had never felt real to me, but through music, it was starting to sink in.

One day, while sitting in my car, I prayed for the courage to make the change. I felt like I could trust Uncle Ray's answers on much of what we had discussed, except for the topic of instrumental music. The CCOC rejection of instrumental music made no sense to me since I was finding so much peace listening to Christian music on the radio. At the same time, I was not ready to risk that much change.

Ready to leave the CCOC and jump ship to the mainstream COC, I called one of the elders at the Clark church. Fear that I would shame my parents and get my dad removed as a church elder at Purling Avenue CCOC if Clark chose to discipline me for leaving riddled me, so I told the elder that my family was going to worship in Columbia instead. I said we would no longer be driving twenty minutes to Clark three times a week. It was a partial truth as I left out the detail about moving over to a mainstream COC.

His kind and understanding reply alleviated my fears, and I felt free. As soon as I turned the radio back on after the call, the Newsboys' song "I Am Free" started. Surely it was a sign. I wept with joy. Could God be speaking to me without my Bible open and with instruments playing in the background? I was amazed.

Still, I was not fully free. The guilt I felt over my hatred for Darius and Northside gnawed at my conscience. One night, I had a nightmare about killing Darius. I would never have done such an evil thing, so why would I dream about it? I was sitting in the bathroom contemplating this question when a verse came to mind: "Everyone who hates his brother is a murderer, and you know that no murderer has eternal life abiding in him" (1 John 3:15).

Overcome with emotion and conviction, I wept and mourned my sin. I prayed for help to love and reconcile, not to be friends with Darius again, but to be kind, cordial, and cooperative. In answer, by God's grace and years of effort on both our parts, we were eventually able to coexist peacefully.

God talking through a dream, a song, or even through what may have been an angel named Larry Justice was not even in the realm of possibility within CCOC beliefs. I had no idea what to think about any of it, but I did feel more loved by my heavenly Father. The God I had known sought to catch me in sin, condemn me, and damn me. The God I was coming to know was reaching out to me, encouraging me, and saving me. It was surreal because I knew deep down I wasn't good enough to deserve any of it. But isn't that the point of the gospel? None of us deserves His love and grace, yet He so freely gives it to us. What good news!

An Unanticipated Affirmation

When the Lowlers and we visited the Parsene Road Church of Christ (a mainstream COC) for the first time, we were pleasantly surprised to hear a lesson on the indwelling of the Holy Spirit. The teacher was an elder at the church, and like nearly all the elders there, he was a gentle, genuine, loving shepherd. Just what the Lowlers and we needed to start this new journey, and maybe, just maybe, these Christians wouldn't judge us for the wine and beer we drank together.

One afternoon, I was sitting in the Parsene Road COC preacher's office explaining a little bit about my issues at Northside. Wilson was a large-framed, animated black minister who was gifted to preach with clarity and passion. The first thing he did upon being called to ministry was to shave his dreadlocks and buy a suit. He was relaxed, down-to-earth, real, and honest, and he helped me realize that I had always seen Jesus through the lens of law, but now I was seeing Him through the lens of grace. He showed me that I had been disappointed by Northside, but now God was reappointing me.

We finished our conversation with a prayer. His large offensive tackle-sized hands engulfed my pale fingers, and we bowed our heads together. As only a theater major and award-winning playwright could do, Wilson affirmed before God to God that I was a child of God. He spoke words of affirmation over me, and I was overwhelmed by my Father's presence, assurance, and love.

We stayed at Parsene Road COC for a few years, and I learned to see God in a much different light. Hope was breaking through.

At the time, I felt like I was on the right track. However, as my heart opened to God's grace and love, I began to lean toward Reformed theology. I loved the folks at Parsene Road and still do. But how could I ever leave the COC?

Chapter 15

NEW NEIGHBORS

I Feel You Slipping Away

I am with you,
But you are not near.

I talk to you,
But I do not hear you respond.

The joyful tones in your voice
Are rarely heard.

Your speech at times is slurred
And filled with thoughtful pauses.

The energetic gleam in your eyes
Is fatigued.

Your confident presence
Makes room for fear.

Your posture
Is stooped in defeat.

"What is wrong with your dad?"
So many have asked,

Only to recount some discouraging tale
Of misspoken words or confused behavior.

Is it so hard to see
Why I am so sad?

I feel you slipping away from me.

IN SCRIPTURE, JESUS announced that He came to earth to give believers an abundant life (John 10:10). He declared that He is the Way, the Truth, and the Life (John 14:6). He also said the truth will set you free (John 8:32). However, until I escaped the CCOC, I never understood those verses. Legalism made my life feel small and impoverished, not abundant. The CCOC's perfectionism enslaved and confined me. There was no freedom there. Yet, throughout my life, I was sure of one thing: Jesus is the Way, the Truth, and the Life. I believed that if I could somehow see Jesus clearly through the thick fog of religion, I might find freedom and an abundant life.

With that desire at the forefront of my mind, I began attending the Bountiful Life (TBL), a Christian men's organization sponsored by the Navigators that exists to transform men into

Christlikeness. They met on Tuesday mornings at 6:00 a.m., and though the morning alarm clock is a hot poker to my ear, I knew surrounding myself with other men who followed Christ would surely aid my journey. We were all seeking Jesus—not religion, not a church, just Jesus. I learned to do a daily AWG (appointment with God) by praying for the Spirit's guidance, reading a short section of the Bible, meditating on the passage, and then journaling what God was revealing to me. Each week, we would meet in small groups and share what God was teaching us.

Having been forbidden by my conscience from attending denominational organizations like Fellowship of Christian Athletes and Christian Medical and Dental Society, I was shocked to find myself in a small group with a Pentecostal, a Baptist, and a liberal Presbyterian. Yet there I was each week, learning from all that God was revealing to us. I found it strange that they were trying to convince me I was indeed saved. After all, I'd grown up with all the right answers. Previously, I would have felt obligated to teach these spiritually lost denominational people how to become true believers in the "one true church." Instead, I now saw the futility all too clearly. I had no answers and no assurance, but God was slowly changing that.

Thus began a spiritual renewal within me through that group, a renewal that continues to this day. I should have been happy to be free of CCOC, but the damage was already done. Reprogramming my mind, heart, and soul to trust God's grace and love was going to be a long, painful journey. Over thirty years of spiritual abuse was not going to be undone by a single prayer, maybe not even a lifetime of prayer. Meanwhile, life marched on, and the burdens in my life grew heavier.

Through the Valley of the Shadow

In January 2007, my father had myelopathy and required an anterior cervical decompression and fusion. It sounded so simple. The surgery went great, but my dad nearly died twice.

After surgery, he lost his airway and required intubation and mechanical ventilation for no apparent reason. Bleeding at the surgery site can compress the airway, but that was not the case for my dad. We had no explanation, and our only hope was to wait. Thankfully, a few days later, he began breathing on his own and was extubated, though still in a comatose state.

Our waiting was in vain. He lost his airway again, aspirated, and was reintubated and placed on a mechanical ventilator for a second time. Due to the aspiration, he developed pneumonia. After what is now considered an outpatient procedure, my father remained an inpatient in the intensive care unit for a week. Again, we had no explanation and no idea what to expect. We prayed, but answers were scarce. Finally, Dad started breathing on his own yet again and was extubated. He remained in the ICU for a couple more days to recover from the pneumonia.

Balancing a busy hip and knee surgical practice and a home with three active children, along with what I thought was a dying parent, had me stretched thin, drawn, and quartered. One arm was pulled toward caring for the next generation, while the other was drawn to the passing generation. One leg was pulled toward work, and the other toward everything else, which included my spiritual struggles. If I hadn't relented about taking an antidepressant again, I'm not sure I would have survived.

It was the darkest time of my life, and it was made even darker by the first postoperative death of my career. The patient was only in his midfifties, and he left behind a loving wife and children, who couldn't comprehend how their dad had suddenly died two days postoperatively. One of his kids was a lawyer, and he was filled with questions. I gave them all the time they needed to ask questions and process what happened late into the night. Eventually, they seemed to come to terms with the uncertainty. I personalized every patient's outcome, whether it was good or bad, so in death, I felt like a complete failure. The sadness in me grew.

After nearly a couple of weeks in the ICU, my dad made it to the hospital floor once he was finally able to protect his airway. However, he could do nothing else. Nothing. He couldn't talk, swallow, or walk. It looked like he wouldn't make it out of the hospital, and his situation remained bleak for days. Thankfully, he was in the same hospital where I worked, so I started every morning by visiting him before making rounds on my own post-op patients. I spent every break between operative cases at his bedside, and every evening, my mother and I were with him. I barely saw my kids except when they came to the hospital to visit "Poppy." This went on for months.

Sherry was my strength, our strength. She was a stay-at-home mom at the time and taught morning aerobics. Thankfully, she had plenty of time to serve our family, though I'm sure her arms were stretched between the generations even more than mine. She ran the kids everywhere, answered all their questions, and still had time to sit with Mom, Dad, and me. Her presence was a powerful force of compassionate love and confident trust in God during those dark days.

Eventually, Dad started talking. Though confused and disoriented, he knew us. Thank God! My mom had been through Alzheimer's with her mother, and over the past several weeks, the one thing that she swore she could not handle was Dad forgetting who she was. Later, Dad had to have a feeding tube placed because he still couldn't swallow. He lay in bed in diapers because he had no bowel control, a catheter for lack of bladder control, and a regimented turning from side to side to prevent bed sores.

Things looked hopeless. We kept praying, but we also started planning. We knew it would be best for Dad to be near all of his physicians, which now included a local neurologist and an internist, both of whom were godsends. We wondered if Dad would ever be able to go back home. If he did, he would need to avoid stairs. The split-level home in Oak Grove was not going to work. What if he never walked again? What if he needed a nursing home?

Crushed with sorrow, we toured the Cliffs, a skilled nursing facility. Mom and I met a nurse, and she walked us around the facility. It was clean, and the people seemed friendly. But the rooms were small and sad, and the cafeteria looked like a gloomy gathering of the lonely and aged. The dementia unit was rock bottom. It was too much.

I still wanted to believe that hope was within reach, but optimism was hard to come by. Was God even listening to our prayers? Had he already made up His mind? What was going to happen to my father? When would I just get a glimpse of improvement? All I needed to see was a little progress in the right direction. Then my hope wouldn't seem so foolish. Then I wouldn't feel so guilty for advocating for the surgery that led to this mess.

A Long Road

The daily grind of work, family, and hospital visits was taking a serious toll. My mother, my wife, and I were all exhausted and felt just about ready to give up. That's when Dad woke up one day without warning. He wasn't out of the woods, but he was able to attempt communication in a garbled, incomprehensible voice. He looked like he'd had a stroke that left him unable to vocalize properly, but countless scans proved otherwise. He started to swallow thickened liquids after a swallowing study proved he could do it without aspirating. Still, he kept the feeding tube in his belly to ensure he got enough nourishment. Although he couldn't verbally communicate it, Dad seemed visibly excited to enjoy his first cup of coffee in months, even if it was thickened and looked like gravy.

Next, my father finally began moving his extremities on his own. Physical and occupational therapists had been gently moving his joints to prevent stiffness, but now they were working on coordinated voluntary movements. Speech therapy worked on swallowing and talking. Slowly, day by day, Dad seemed to be improving.

Once Dad started talking comprehensibly, we discovered that he was definitely not himself. In his post-ICU delirium, he considered us all damnable players on the stage of his miserable life, all except Sherry, whom he referred to as "pussycat." She could do no wrong, but the rest of us had him worried. It was too funny not to laugh, at least for Sherry and me. Dad was convinced that my mom was having an affair—a lesbian affair, no less. He just couldn't believe that after over forty years of marriage, Mom had turned out to be a lesbian.

He also couldn't stop worrying about Dan's gambling. He was convinced Dan was going to lose his house to gambling debt. Try as we might to divert conversations, he kept returning to his false beliefs. Dan didn't mind that Dad thought he was too leveraged, but my mom was grieved that Dad would ever question her faithfulness. Just hearing the bizarre accusation wounded her.

We received a clue to his true diagnosis when he began having hallucinations. It was tragic, though at times darkly amusing. We'd be sitting in the room talking, and Dad would jump like he'd seen a ghost. It never failed to startle me. He would jump, and then I would jump even higher before either of us knew what had happened. I was too anxious to laugh at it, but Sherry got a kick out of the drama. Dad was seeing people, car wrecks, and animals, where we saw only blank walls.

As it turns out, this is exactly what Lewy body dementia does to a person, but we still assumed it was post-ICU psychosis.

Gradually, his coordination began to return. When Dad took his first steps after not walking for over a month, we celebrated with tears of joy. He was an uncoordinated mess, but he was moving his legs. His arms and hands were a different story. We continued to feed him, wipe his nose, and help him use the bathroom. I will never forget the feeling of complete humility when I helped him with his bowel movement while my mom was taking a much-needed break. That's how I learned for the first time that my father was uncircumcised. It was a surreal experience that was only outmatched by a visit from his occupational therapist, Dottie.

It was now Valentine's Day, which meant he'd been in the hospital for six weeks. Dottie came into the room to help him make a Valentine's Day card for my mom. *You have got to be kidding,* I thought, as she carried in a tub of arts-and-crafts supplies similar to the one we had at home for our kids (which they had outgrown years ago). Dottie got out some construction paper and let Dad choose a color. My dad still couldn't wipe his runny nose. How was he going to make a greeting card?

As Dottie squirted glue onto a sheet of construction paper and guided my dad's hands to spread it, she explained what a good tactile experience this was for him. But all I saw was a degrading display of helplessness. She had him sprinkle glitter and use some markers. When he was done, his card looked like a toddler had made it, but Dottie was satisfied with the therapy session and left. Sherry and I were the only ones watching, and we were heartbroken. Then he surprised us. His nose was runny again, and suddenly, he reached for a tissue and wiped his own nose. It was a miracle! Apparently, Dottie knew what she was doing.

Slowly, Dad improved. He began talking more clearly, and his walking improved. The swallowing problem persisted, so he continued to be fed through his G-tube. His self-care also slowly improved, and he eventually made enough progress to warrant a transfer to Columbia Regional Hospital's rehabilitation unit, where he received excellent care. By then, Mom had been living with us for eight or ten weeks, and I hadn't spent even one evening at home with my kids.

Mentally, I was doing better thanks to Wellbutrin. It gave me headaches and insomnia, but at least I didn't feel like I was circling the drain of despair. God was propping me up so I could be strong for my parents in their time of great need, but my knees were getting weak. I had not yet learned to share my burdens with Jesus, so each day seemed overwhelming. We had to make some major decisions without the patriarch's blessing, which was a major CCOC no-no. Were we not going to wait until Dad became completely lucid to make decisions that would affect the rest of his life? What if he never became lucid?

The problem was that he couldn't go home to a house with stairs, but at least it looked like he was going to escape rehab soon. If he went home to Oak Grove, he would have all new doctors, and I would have no influence. But if he moved to Columbia, where would my parents live? How would Dan feel about having his dad move away after finally arriving back home to the Kansas City area? Could they afford to move? Could they sell their house?

At that point in my life, trusting God was not a concept I understood. I was raised the CCOC way, which was to pull myself up by my own bootstraps. I had to figure this out on my own and fix it.

Little did I know, God was already making a way. A house in my neighborhood, just one block away, went on the market. It was a slab home with three bedrooms and no stairs, and it was within eyesight of our home. The Oak Grove house sold quickly to some lifelong friends, and rather than feeling animosity, Dan generously packed up the old house and even provided the moving trucks.

By the summer of 2007, things were looking up. I felt good enough to stop my Wellbutrin after six months. I thought I was cured. Dad was settled into Columbia, and I believed I was ready for whatever lay ahead.

Chapter 16

LIFE LOOKS GOOD
ON THE OUTSIDE

Loss

His ashen face concealed the usual joyful expression.
All lines, tubes, and monitors removed,
He now lay unresponsive,
Warmed only by the tears and soft whispers of his wife's last
embrace.

What could I say as I sat and held her hand in the night hours
Waiting for her family to arrive?
What could I do but silently look from her to him?
I prayed for wisdom and strength
Only to feel helpless and alone.

"He loves me so much,"
She confessed with confidence.
His love comforted her.

But then she painfully recalled,
"We do everything together.
We go for walks, we shop, we do everything—together!"

Their love was once forbidden by difference,
Yet he faithfully returned for her after the war.
Bravely, she left her wealthy Vietnamese family
And built her own beautiful family.

One last breath,
One last movement,
Valiant efforts ensued to no avail.
A beautiful family forever changed.

I helplessly stood by
Watching him fight back with faint signs of life.
Then death finally won.
I failed.
The burnout was complete.

I am spent.
I pray for strength.
Christ meets me in communion and gently whispers,
"It's OK. Everything is going to be all right."
A shepherd places his hand gently on my shoulder
And I struggle to die to self to serve another day.

WITH MY FATHER and mother settled into their new home, life seemed to be heading in the right direction. From the outside, it must have looked like I had it all, and for the most part, I did. My surgical practice was busy and thriving. I had performed over a thousand joint replacements, and most seemed to do quite well. God blessed my years of learning with both clinical and financial success. We remodeled our house and added a sunroom and a swimming pool. We were vacationing several times a year at the beach and in the mountains.

I'd started my career in Columbia needing orthodontic braces, and I finally had the juvenile ceramic braces removed from my teeth. For the first time in my life, I was proud of my smile. My kids were healthy and content in school. My wife was free, fun, and available. Dad was improving. Everything seemed great.

Spiritually, I was growing in grace through TBL and Parsene Road COC. Around this time, Kyle Brooks, my Pentecostal TBL friend, recommended a book to me. The book was Sam Storms's *Singing God: Discover the Joy of Being Enjoyed by God*. I read it and reread it and found within its pages a God who is passionately in love with me. He didn't seem angry or disappointed at all. Just like me at bedtime with my kids, He sings over me, rejoices over me, and even delights in me. It all sounded way too good to be true. Still, I was starting to doubt my doubts about Him.

Quickening the pace of my spiritual journey into God's love, my family and I went to our first Zoe Conference in Nashville, Tennessee, that autumn. The theme was "Overflow," and for two days, I soaked in the Bible's teaching on God's love and unmerited favor in my life. It truly felt like God was singing over me. For the first time in my life, I worshipped the Triune God with uplifted hands and a heart that overflowed with His love. A passion for His grace ignited within me.

When I returned home, I was convinced that I should give up my medical career to become a minister. I had to do something big for God because I was finally seeing that He had done something immeasurably good for me. Foolishly, I was intent on earning God's unmerited favor.

Despite my growing awareness of God's grace, anxiety and fear continued to stir within my unmedicated mind. I so desperately wanted to give my children a better life, but I was too hard on them. I feared they would end up rebellious like me, and that, unlike me, they might not come back home. So I disciplined them out of fear. I directed and commanded them out of fear. I could lead us into a beautiful Norman Rockwell-like moment and, minutes later, explode in anger. I was volatile. In an attempt to gain control of my anger, I began reading the book *Anger Is a Choice* by Dr. Tim LaHaye and Bob Phillips, but it made me so angry and anxious that I couldn't finish it.

Trying to work on my anger got me nowhere. On the contrary, my anger got worse. A big contributing factor was the orthopaedic pain that was beginning to dominate my life. In the summer of 2007, I made my second appearance on the other side of the orthopaedic table. (I had a right wrist ganglion cyst removed during residency.) By then, standing on my right foot had become unbearable despite nonoperative treatment, and my left shoulder was in the same boat. After more than a year of treatment, on the weekend before Independence Day, I had shoulder and foot surgery at the same time so I could recover quickly over the holiday and get back to work. What a mistake! My foot wound opened up a month later, right before Sherry and I were all set to go to Cap Juluca to celebrate our fifteenth wedding anniversary. Fortunately, we managed to have a magical time that was only occasionally interrupted by packing my foot wound.

The magic ended on the drive home from the airport when I felt the sudden urge to use the restroom. I barely made it to a Walmart stall in time to unleash my bowels. By the time we got home, I had 102-degree fever, which remained for two weeks, along with diarrhea that lasted six months. Numerous trips to a gastroenterologist along with multiple negative stool sample tests scared me. I felt like I was dying. In desperation, I humbly called the Parsene Road elders to come pray over me. The day after their prayers, my fever broke, and I finally was able to return to work. God's grace had never felt so real.

Yet, in addition to managing chronic diarrhea, I was also battling back pain, which started the day I stood up from my research desk during my fellowship and felt what seemed like a hot poker in my butt cheek. I misdiagnosed myself with sacro-iliac joint pain and treated it with physical therapy to stabilize my pelvis. The pain improved with core strengthening, only to recur often enough during the beginning years of practice at the Columbia Orthopaedic Group that I finally asked a spine surgeon partner what could be wrong with me.

He told me it was a classic case of a herniated lumbar disk and gave me an epidural steroid injection, which was almost as magical as Cap Juluca. I was amazed at the relief. Still, I was afraid of the diagnosis and didn't want to confirm it with an MRI. I chose to bury my head in the sand rather than accept that my back was on its way to becoming like my dad's. It wasn't until my senior total joint partner asked me, in a not-so-gentle way, "Why would you want to work so hard only to find out later that you have cancer in your back?" The *C* word scared me, and I got the MRI that day. It revealed that I had a collapsed L5-S1 disk space. There was no cancer. I was all set to continue working too hard.

No Escape

Busyness is all I knew. Years earlier, I had been elected by my partners to sit on the executive committee. I took my role as head of the personnel committee very seriously and was able to transition our employees to an "earned time off" benefits package, along with a bonus system. Though I was busy building my surgical practice to four hundred joint replacements per year, I was not content to only be a part of the Columbia Orthopaedic Group. I worked hard to make a positive impact on its culture. Later, I would take on the role of chief of the Boone Hospital Center's Orthopaedic Department. I had plenty of irons in the fire.

To add to that, my parents now lived in town, and I had to figure out the extent of my role in their lives. Should I visit every day? Would Mom be lonely while Dad continued to recover at home? Should we eat meals together once a week? Twice? Rather than asking them, I wore myself out trying to anticipate their needs, constantly playing the role of fixer.

The undercurrent, dragging me into depression, grew stronger. My recovery and rehabilitation from surgery was slow and tiresome. Parenting was becoming more challenging as the kids approached middle school. My anxiety, fear, and anger led to some screaming at home, but thankfully never to physical violence. The verbal abuse I dished out on occasion left me feeling like a constant failure as a dad and as a human being. Yet I was flourishing in my roles at work and church. I was ordained as a deacon in the fall of 2007 and went right to work making the worship as authentic and moving as I felt God deserved. Everything looked great on the surface, but internally, I was struggling to stay above water.

Thankfully, a new drug that promised to help with depression and pain was approved for use. After acquiring a sample pack and trying a few days under my internist's direction, I gave up on it because of night terrors and went back to what had worked previously, Wellbutrin. However, the headaches, insomnia, and fatigue from Wellbutrin proved too much to bear this time, so

I soon gave up treatment, resigning myself to trying harder to be less anxious and depressed.

I was stuck in an endless cycle of giving up and trying harder, but I didn't know what to make of it. I had never heard of such a cycle. I knew one thing for sure: I was ashamed of myself. I couldn't understand why I lacked the faith and willpower to improve. I projected an image of a maturing Christian deacon who overflowed with grace, but it didn't match the shameful sadness I felt inside. It may have seemed like I had it all, but I felt like a fraud. Surely someone as spiritual as I should not battle mental illness.

I should have been "anxious for nothing," as the Scripture says, but I struggled with so many things, even trying to please God with my growing income; it was a mixed blessing for a per-fectionist. I enjoyed wealth, no doubt, but was I saving enough, investing wisely, giving generously, and giving to the right people and organizations? Trying to steward my money tortured me.

My biggest concern at the time was that I was still support-ing CCOC missionaries in Africa. One of them, who had been stabbed in the neck during a carjacking earlier in his life and was a quadraplegic, had just adopted an orphan. Yet his monthly updates were full of familiar stories of CCOC's harsh child-rearing. It made me nauseous. After an exchange of emails with the missionary, I discerned that he was spiritually hurting more people than he was helping. I finally cut off my support to the CCOC missionaries, which also made me anxious because it severed all my ties to the CCOC, except for my connection to my parents.

My primary coping mechanism was to escape on vacation. The year 2008 was chock-full of these escapes. We started out in Disney World for a winter family vacation. We had a blast at three parks with fastpasses timed perfectly through my hours of preparation. Then, in February, wedding bells rang for Sherry's mom and a retired Southern Baptist pastor from North Dakota.

In keeping with my religious work ethic, I planned a church ski trip to Weston, Missouri, which went so badly for my oldest that he temporarily swore off skiing. In March, Sherry and I, along with Mason and his wife, Donna, took a business trip to San Francisco, complete with a side trip in a convertible along the coast past Pebble Beach to Carmel. Back then, the implant reps could foot the bill for nice, expensive meals, so we took advantage of that.

For spring break, I took the family to the Canyons in Utah to get private ski lessons. Thankfully, Spencer changed his mind about skiing. Summer brought piano recitals, Brownies, pool parties, and state championship Little League games for Alex. On our yearly summer trip to Pawley's Island, South Carolina, we took my mom and dad along. Though not without problems, we had a terrific time celebrating the fact that my dad could actually take a trip to the beach. It was his last vacation.

At the end of the summer, we drove with friends to Vail, Colorado, for a guys' mountain biking trip. I had become obsessed with the sport as another way of coping with stress, and Vail was about as good as it gets. After Christmas, we went to Deer Valley, Utah, to ski again.

Battles on All Fronts

Thanks in part to my keen ability to focus on the negative, the rest of that year was filled with a lot of loneliness and pain. Sherry was starting to get busy in her new career as an interior decorator, but we still managed to have our weekly lunches together on clinic days. Our best friends, the Lowlers, moved to Kansas City, leaving a void in our lives. My TBL small group was helpful spiritually, but we never developed any friendships outside of Wednesday mornings. My shoulder and foot continued to bother me for the first half of the year. Then I started having neck pain. A cervical spine MRI showed a couple of levels of degenerative disks. I began to wonder why God would create me to be an orthopaedic surgeon, only to give me so many orthopaedic issues. On the bright side, I developed a strong empathy for my patients after being on the other side. Despite all the time away, I still managed to perform 407 joint replacements that year in the one OR that the hospital allotted to me. Most total joint surgeons operate using two rooms. In fact, that is all I'd known throughout my training.

Between work, church, and recreation, I ran myself ragged. This may have been when I first started experiencing burnout. I didn't know what I was feeling. I just knew I needed to escape. Mountain biking had been a thrilling outlet, but I had to slow it down because of the chronic pain. I had already given up golf because of my shoulder. I couldn't run because of my back. Rather than exercise, I just read more and drank a little more. My mind could not be still.

Money was a constant source of my racing thoughts. Was I a good enough steward? Did I invest in the right places? What if I was missing out on something huge? That last one got me into trouble with my temporary multimillionaire real estate mogul friend, Charleston. I had been on his case to find me a great investment opportunity, and he finally came up with Old Albatross Estates, a fifty-nine-acre tract of land that appraised for $2.5 million with only a $1.4 million purchase price and mortgage. He was going to let me buy in as a one-ninth partner. We expected to flip it quickly and deliver the windfall we needed to buy a large apartment complex and create steady passive income. Charleston had houses in Columbia, Sanibel Island, and Vail, two airplanes, and more. I was convinced he knew the path to riches, so I hitched my wagon to his. When he said to buy Premier Bank shares, I bought $54,000 worth.

Then the real estate market bubble burst. Sadly, the global financial crisis devastated Charleston. He was leveraged to the gills and lost nearly everything. And I soon learned what joint and several meant when the bank looked to me to pay the mortgage note on Old Albatross. We had speculated on an overvalued piece of dirt, devoid of income-producing potential and a viable sewer utility option. Naturally, the bank called the note, reappraised the property at a value below loan value, and then demanded more collateral.

Slowly and with great mental agony on everyone's part, I became the majority shareholder of Old Albatross with only one other partner remaining who could pay on the note. That other partner used to have 33.3 percent but agreed to stay in at 25 percent. Within a matter of months, I went from paying one-ninth of the note to paying 75 percent. To pour a little salt into the wound, Premier Bank failed, rendering my shares worthless. Financially, the only bright spot that year was that my partners and I at the Columbia Orthopaedic Group finished a new state-of-the-art seventy-two-thousand-square-foot building, complete with an ambulatory surgery center, which was sure to bring in more than enough ancillary income to cover my losses.

Financial pressure was not the only force closing in on me. I spent the summer TBL session reading and studying what the Bible has to say on sexual purity. The Holy Spirit had some work to do. God needed to change my heart to get the occasional pornography out of my life. Nothing I had tried worked. I had to learn to trust God that concealing sin leads to ruin and that healing only comes by confession. What was I to do? I thought

I would melt if I told a soul about my secret sin, but how could I be a child of God and still go on sinning as if His sacrifice meant nothing to me?

A Glimpse of Light in the Darkness

By October 2008, I was not doing well despite all the vacations. We went to our second Zoe conference in Nashville, this time with Sherry's brother's family. The theme was "Fearless," which seemed perfectly timed by God. Before the conference, I had read and fallen in love with the God described in *The Shack*. At the conference, a man spoke in detail about the book and about coming to terms with our anger at God for bad events in our lives. In a sense, as the preacher put it, I needed to "forgive" God for the past. I thought this might be a new beginning, but the past spiritual lies and the present burnout kept pulling me under.

In desperation, I tried Cymbalta again, hoping it would help some of the neck and back pain along with the looming depression. However, after a few months of night terrors, I once again swore off all medication for mental health. I decided to conquer this giant on my own. Maybe God would help, or maybe not—I couldn't tell.

Desperate for a break, my mind swam laps in the pools of Calvinism, Arminianism, church orthodoxy, and orthopraxy. Something had to give. I needed a change. One afternoon while mountain biking, I cried out to God, pleading with Him to bring a good Christian friend into my life. I must have looked like a fool standing beside my bike in the middle of the woods, sobbing and screaming. But God answered. Not long after, He brought James Sweet and his family into our lives. James was an elder at Garth Avenue Church. We visited his church several times, loved it, and grew to love the Sweets as well.

Moving along the Restoration Movement spectrum, we finally decided it was time for me to resign as a deacon and join the Garth Avenue Church, which sang and played the same songs that encouraged us on the radio. Our kids were in the vulnerable preteen and teenage years, and they needed a strong youth group.

We loved it. My dad, on the other hand, did not. When I told him, he flung himself back in his recliner with his arms and legs outstretched like a starfish, as if he had just been drawn and quartered. It was actually quite astonishing. Unlike my dad, my Uncle Ray was "very proud" of me for making the change, and it felt great to hear him say so.

Trying to learn better boundaries, I promised myself I wouldn't serve in the church for at least one year. Work was going to be different, too. No more cycling in and out of burnout. I was determined to take Fridays off and limit my clinic. My back needed more rest, so I had to slow down every part of my life. But how could I slow down when I had the Old Albatross mortgage to pay? Somehow, I had to get my eyes off myself and onto Jesus, and I hoped the new church would show me the way. I wanted to experience Jesus's abundant life, a life of freedom, a life free from shame and perfectionism.

Meeting the Sweets topped off the year with a happy note. The first night we double-dated together, we laughed until our stomachs hurt. They were proper, and we were a little more off-color than they were used to. What attracted us to them was their joy. They seemed like they had it together. James had been an elder in the church since he was thirty years old. He and Tina had been hosting the high school youth group for decades. Their four children were a few years older than ours and seemed to be on fire for Jesus. So not only did we have a ton of fun with them, but also their lives were simply attractive. I wanted the joy and peace that they had.

We finished off the year with eight Christmas trees in our house, each with a different theme. Sherry had discovered a hidden talent for home decor. At our annual Christmas party, she showcased what she could do, and it was breathtaking.

Chapter 17

HEALING BEGINS

I Live to Worship Him

Guilt shackled my life
But grace unleashed peace
From the bonds of fear
Freedom brought release

Filled with the Holy Spirit
Joy reigns in my heart
I live to worship
In life set apart.

I live to worship
Jesus, my King
I live to praise Him

He is all that I am
He is all that I have
He is all that I need

He's my Savior and
I live to worship Him

WITH NEW FRIENDS and a new church, I entered 2009 full of hope. My first journal entry of the year reads like a manic episode. After several pages of brainstorming and planning all my ideas of "doing something *big*" to show my love for God, I wrote the following:

> To make a difference, one must leave a legacy! A legacy would inspire my children to make a difference! This is precisely the legacy I'd like to leave! If a boy with a brain tumor can create an orphanage in Africa, what will I be responsible for? God, please bless me with a vision to commit to, an idea You inspire, a work that brings glory to You from the bounty with which You've blessed me!

Energized by a better understanding of God and His love, I wanted to make Him proud. The surgery center was bringing in money, along with the imaging center, durable medical equipment, and real estate revenue streams, and I was determined to make an impact for Christ's kingdom with my money.

I toyed with the idea of starting a tuition-free music school for the poor, or maybe an orphanage, a homeless shelter, a mountain bike park, or a refugee center. I also wanted to start an Oak Grove Scholarship in my parents' name, which my mom and I eventually did, and named it the Hockman Hardware

Scholarship. Clearly, my mind was racing. Even so, at the time I took no action because I questioned if all these grand ideas were from God or from me, for God or for me. My desire to leave a Hockman legacy answered the question for me.

I was learning from the Garth Street church, as well as my own personal reading of twenty or thirty Christian books a year, that God was so much more than I had ever known (and undoubtedly more than I ever could know). Filled with a sense of God's grace and love, I still felt like I should be doing more. Everyone around me was so enthusiastic about Jesus and involved in doing so many things for Him. Though I kept my commitment not to teach or lead, I plunged into activities and programs. The kids attended youth group while we attended a Sunday school class. Sunday night was time for more youth group activities. Alex, Paige, and I all participated in the church musical, Camp HolloCrawla. We were having a great but busy time.

After two months at Garth Street, I was feeling good. The depressed mood had lifted from my weary mind. Much of my chronic pain seemed to have vanished. I was sleeping well again and felt rested and at peace with myself and God. For perhaps the first time in my life, I felt alive in Christ. Still, I worried that the old path of seeking status and approval in church could continue to enslave me to a performance-based religion. As I was trying to show more grace to myself, I naturally extended the same to others. Garth Street was a nondenominational church that sought to include Christians from all backgrounds, whether Catholic, Orthodox, or some variant of Protestant. The CCOC burden of "saving" all the "lost" Christians was lifted. I was starting to get a taste of freedom. Now I could make spiritual connections with as many patients as were willing by praying with them and feeling mutually encouraged.

Though the idea that God could actually smile at me now rang true, my unrepentant and unconfessed sin still weighed me down. Being formed into Christ's image seemed like an impossible task. I kept trying harder and harder, only to fail again and again. Scripture teaches that righteousness comes from God, not from within ourselves, but I couldn't quite stop looking within.

The lack of moral perfection obscured the good I was accomplishing at home and work. Theoretically, my family was now free from the CCOC, but I was still hindered by moralism. Ultimately, God was opening the gate to the pathway of trusting in Him, not in me, but I hadn't gone through it completely yet.

Learning to Lean on Jesus

Sin wasn't the only road block to trusting God. The American healthcare system practically paralyzed me in a state of rage and anxiety. Once again, inner peace was fleeting. It is impossible to overstate how much damage governmental interference did to the profession of medicine during my career through unrelenting storms of regulations, increased costs, and decreased reimbursement. The modern American healthcare system seemed to accuse physicians of being a greedy, self-centered, system abuser, rather than a conscientious caregiver. My back pain had returned, and I was burned out again, only this time I was turning to an occasional double of scotch to self-medicate.

The roller coaster of emotional instability continued even though God was blessing my surgical practice with good outcomes and a growing reputation, as well as blessing my home with a healthy, mostly happy family. However, because of my tireless hard work, sacrifice, and charitable giving, I felt God owed me more. I should not have to deal with all of this back and leg pain. I was doing my part with physical therapy, but I felt like God owed me some pain relief. What's more, I thought my wife should be listening to me more, complimenting me more, showing me more affection, and keeping the house and finances in better order. And the kids should be more respectful to me, kinder to each other, and more obedient and appreciative. As a result of these unattainable expectations, I was looking everywhere except God for validation, which left me depressed, again.

The cycle of burnout and recovery was a constant in my life. I was ashamed of it. It made me feel like a failure. A Calvinist friend at work counseled me that I was "living too much in the flesh." Dr. Byron White was a general surgeon who read theology books between cases in the surgeons' lounge. He was about twenty years older than me and took an interest in my faith journey. He seemed more at peace than any Christian I had ever met, and I wondered what he was learning from all his study. In a simple act of kindness, he gave me *God's Ultimate Purpose: An Exposition on Ephesians 1* by Dr. Martyn Lloyd-Jones. After reading only the first half, I encountered a beautiful view of God.

I wanted more, but at times, a couple drinks just seemed easier. Physically, it seemed like harmless drinking in moderation, but spiritually, I was still self-condemning because my upbringing had taught me that even a drop on the tongue was sinful. Never mind that Jesus taught that it is what comes out of the heart that defiles, not what goes into the stomach. Never mind that Jesus turned water into wine. In my mind, I was skating on thin ice with God, so I decided to fast from alcohol to spend more time praying about it (or perhaps more truthfully, obsessing over it).

Ultimately, I concluded that God was not trying to withhold good from me, but rather to bless me with a clean conscience. Jeremiah 29:11 seemed like the answer I was looking for ("'For I know the plans I have for you,' declares the Lord, 'plans for your welfare and not for evil, to give you a future and a hope.'"), so I decided once and for all to give up alcohol for my good Father.

That same month, I was served with a frivolous lawsuit, something that nearly every doctor faces at some point. The timing was sublime. My back pain was getting the best of me, despite having just had my ninth or tenth epidural steroid injection. I tried Neurontin, which caused an adverse reaction of diarrhea and a rash—a perfect combo when trying to operate on people. Elavil at night helped some, but I still suffered. A nice glass of cabernet would have helped, but I resisted the urge and made a clear decision to let go of any anxiety about the lawsuit. I had done nothing wrong and refused to let it get to me. By now, I was tiptoeing through the open gate toward trusting God, and it brought peace about the situation.

Still, the real battle lay before me. Could I trust God with confessing my secret sin? The answer came through my Garth Street Men's group. I had developed a close relationship with three guys in the group who had been kind enough to include me earlier in the year. This group went deeper than "news, weather, and sports." They held each other accountable to being loyal to King Jesus, and that included sexual purity. After being convinced that I was not alone, God finally gave me the courage to take another step toward trusting Him.

One Wednesday in August, no one could make it to the men's group except the group leader and me. After a brief discussion on whatever it was we were reading together, I finally confessed my secret sin. I was so nervous that I don't remember how I brought it up or what I said, but for the first time in my thirty-eight years of life, I told another person that I occasionally used pornography to cope with stress.

Filled with a sudden release of guilt and shame, I wept. He let me know that I was not alone and that everyone in our men's group fought the same battle. He had resisted for over five years after his confession. Transparency brought hope, confession brought healing, and accountability brought honesty. For the first time, I felt like I was on the right track spiritually, yet even as I write this, the shame returns and causes me chest pain and anxiety.

One step remained: confessing to my wife. I knew she would hate me and feared she might leave me. It was just too awful to imagine. Maybe all I needed was to be held accountable to my men's group. Surely, I thought, that was all the repentance God needed from me. Everyone's wife in the men's group knew their husbands' truth but mine. I had two male friends outside of the men's group who went with me to Garth Street, and I found the courage to talk to them about my dilemma. Their wives knew, too. God's will seemed clear. His timing, however, did not—not until October.

Unburdened

Despite having left the Churches of Christ, we still decided to go to our third Zoe conference in Nashville in October. *Inside Out* was the theme. It was too much of a spiritual high to miss, but only Sherry and I could attend. The kids stayed home this time.

We made it as far as St. Louis before the bomb dropped.

Driving past a strip club, I jokingly said that we should go in together. Then, from out of the blue, my wife asked me if I'd ever been inside one. Lying would have kicked the can down the road and made for a more peaceful conference, but I chose to come clean.

"Yes."

"When?"

"When my coresidents took that trip to Dallas for the pros-thetics course. They all went without me, but I was curious and went on my own."

"Did you touch them?"

"No. I was embarrassed and ashamed and left within a matter of minutes."

"What else are you not telling me?"

"Nothing."

I was done for the time being. We fought or sat in silence for the next six hours of the road trip. She couldn't help asking more questions like *Why? Am I not enough? Are you having an affair?* The worship that evening left us feeling empty and straining to connect to God and each other. The next morning we went to the conference and left to grab Panera salads and rehash our road trip because we certainly weren't getting anything out of the conference. We felt drained and went back to our hotel room.

In the hotel room, I began crying like I had never cried before. Looking back, it was the same as when my father passed away. I was broken, completely devastated, and overwhelmed with shame. Even in the face of the dishonesty that Sherry had just uncovered, she still managed to go straight to her "sweet mommy" voice and asked, "Baby, what's wrong?"

"There is more that I'm not telling you," I confessed.

And with that, I told her about using pornography as a way to cope with stress ever since I was a young teenager. With that revelation, her avalanche of questions crushed me with unbearable shame. I deserved it and more. All I could do was be completely calm, open, and honest about what a worthless fraud I was. Truth be told, I had robbed her of being my one and only and traded our oneness for private intimacy with whoever was on screen. I violated her. I violated us.

Her response was shocking, completely surreal, and entirely unexpected. She held me as I sobbed with grief over my sins, my lies, my mask, my shame. She consoled me and told me she wanted to make love to me. My confusion did not prevent us from being together that afternoon, but it did shatter my understanding of what love truly is.

Love is forgiving and comforting someone who has grievously sinned against you, while not knowing whether or not that person will continue to hurt you. To me, love had always seemed conditioned on right behavior, especially God's love. To Sherry, love was obviously not merit-based. Her response left me feeling what my soul had longed for my entire life—accepted for who I was and loved anyway. She knew the authentic me and loved me. She knew what Jesus knew, that I am more than my sin, and she inspired me to change my view of myself. Yet, the scars of shame are deep and do not easily fade.

All I'd ever really wanted was to feel good enough to be loved, but inside I knew I would never measure up to God's perfect standard. In the past, when I'd been caught for shameful behavior, I had been slapped in the face. Yet, Sherry chose to be Jesus to me. I had confessed to her what I had hidden from her for twenty years, and she ran to me like the Father running to the prodigal son. She was filled with unconditional love, forgiveness, and grace, and she chose to love me at my lowest point. She showed me God's love.

Chapter 18

RECOVERY

Let Me Be Loved

Let your love fall down on me gently
  Like snowflakes on Lake Champetra
For I am weak and fragile
  And find it hard to receive love
Let your presence surround me slowly
  Like smoke billowing from a fire
For I am unworthy of your holy touch
  And find the gift of your presence overwhelming
Let me hear you say again, "I love you"
  Then I will believe it was You and not me
Let me sense calm assurance of trust
  And know my fleeting contentment need not depart
Let fear loosen its grip
  On my every thought, my every moment
Heal me, Father, of the sickness
  That whispers I am not good enough

Heal me, Jesus, of the past
    That preached you are not enough
Heal me, Spirit, of the darkness
    That shadows Your light in my soul
Truth, God, show me how to take hold
    Of the truth that I am Yours
Make me at peace in Your loving presence
    Let me be loved

OUR FRIENDS, THE Sweets, walked beside us throughout the process of sorting out our emotions. They had been through the same trauma and were invaluable in helping us along our journey to freedom from secrecy and shame. What incredible friends, what amazing love! They listened and offered gentleness, kindness, and grace. They mediated with understanding. We will forever be thankful.

The next few months weren't easy. Questions constantly arose from Sherry's doubting mind. I offered answers and reassurance that I loved her, found her attractive, and had never physically betrayed her. I had never and would never, but she needed time to sort through her doubts. It got tiresome being under the microscope constantly, but I deserved worse and was thankful that she still loved me. I loved her more than ever.

Unlike the Sweets, I had been a huge hypocrite when we'd seen two other couples deal with the same issue at the CCOC. To my shame, I remained silent about my sin. The difference between those men and me was that I had confessed, and they had been caught in the act. I had always known I had a sin problem and desperately wanted help. It may not have been an addiction in the truest sense of the word, but it was a sinful habit that stared accusingly at me for most of my life, mocking my faith and my sanity. So I finally sought some answers to the deep questions of why. Why was I this way? If I couldn't figure out what to do with my past, then I knew I would be bound to repeat it.

A Google search on "Christian counseling," along with advice from a friend, directed me to Bryce Roland, a licensed clinical counselor at New Life Christian Counseling Center. For the next two years, Bryce listened and offered wisdom that changed the trajectory of my life. To me, he was an apostle and prophet, one sent who speaks for God. We met seven times during the next two months. To use a worn-out cliché, it was like drinking water from a fire hydrant, but it didn't start that way.

For our first meeting, we met in an old office lined with books and sat in chairs angled toward each other to seem less confrontational. However, my opening line was a bit harsh, as if we were seated across a desk from each other, me in a high-backed banker's office chair and him in a grade-school plastic chair. I didn't mean for it to come across as hostile, and fortunately, Bryce didn't take it that way.

What I said was, "How is it possible for me to talk about a personal problem and then listen to your response and have any of it make any difference in my life?"

I was unintentionally, arrogantly skeptical that he could help such a brilliant thinker as I. He quickly proved me wrong, and I wound up hanging onto every word, taking notes when I got home to remind me of his wisdom.

He first asked me why I had come to him. Not wanting to waste any time or money, I quickly told him about my confession in Nashville. He then began to unpack my life story one question at a time, offering some interpretation along the way. He told me unhealthy habits are essentially idols that let us temporarily cope with and escape from something painful in life. What I needed to do was to determine what I was trying to escape. As I listened, I was riddled with anxiety, which manifested as chest pain. Bryce rightfully pointed out that I was actually overcome with fear. But what was I afraid of?

Upon further probing, he realized I had some unhealthy misconceptions about who God is. I wanted to punish myself for my sin until God could accept me again. Shockingly (and I'll never forget this, even without the notes), Bryce explained that God does indeed have preferences about my behavior, but He loves me regardless of my behavior. I couldn't accept this truth because it didn't feel right to me.

Bryce showed me that truth filtered through beliefs gives rise to feelings. I had wrong feelings because I had wrong beliefs. Apparently, it turned out, some beliefs may not be helpful and can, in fact, become harmful. He later described our beliefs as "old tapes" that are constantly running in the background of our minds, either helping or distorting reality.

One of my unhealthy false beliefs was that God was an angry, demanding tyrant. No wonder I lived with fear. I appreciated Bryce's response to my view of God.

"Know that God's love," he said, "like your love for your kids, is unconditional. Nothing can separate you from God's love. Stop punishing yourself and be blessed by God. You wouldn't want your kids to beat themselves up, would you? So make yourself available to God so that He is blessed. It's like when my three-year-old daughter sees me sitting in the living room and jumps up on my lap to snuggle. As her father, I'm blessed by that, but she had to make herself available to me. God wants you to do the same."

It was a beautiful image, but the old tapes don't erase easily.

I used to joke that my parents seemed to have more unconditional love than God did, but through the counseling experience, I became disappointed and angry with my parents for taking me to a church that taught me such a damning view of God. Bryce often quoted John's gospel about the importance of bringing truth to light. Well, one truth is that I had always been a fearful people-pleaser, hoping by chance that I might even please God. Bryce helped me see that I needed to learn to be a son of God, which meant peace and joy in my life, not fear and anxiety.

To start, I needed to forgive my parents, even though they were stuck in the CCOC movement and may never change. He taught me that forgiveness is a process unrelated to the offender's behavior.

In one session, my world had been turned upside down (or more aptly, right side up). Bryce had challenged my view of God, my parents, my sin, and my past, and it had huge implications for my future. It simultaneously sounded too good to be true and too scary to imagine. Bryce left me with the goal just to make progress each day. Perfection cannot be obtained, but progress can.

Four days later, we met again and discussed my childhood relationships with my parents, brother, and peers. It was a day of discovery as I realized the dysfunction in my family. My constant spankings were more punishment than discipline. Also, I was taught that protecting the family name was of primary importance. My sophomoric alcohol problem was possibly a subconscious effort to be caught in rebellion to bring down the family name. However, the most significant discovery was that I had been spiritually abused.

Spiritual Abuse

Spiritual abuse occurs when someone in authority uses their position to harm your relationship with God for their own gain.

That pretty well describes a church that scoffs at even the idea of a personal relationship with God. CCOC was not all bad. I received some good beliefs from them, but unfortunately, I received them in a harmful way.

This discovery further fueled my resentment toward my parents. How could I reconcile the mountains of scriptural knowledge, the ability to study Scripture, and a love for the Bible that I learned from my parents with the church that had pushed me farther from God and prevented me from having a relationship with the source of all that wisdom and knowledge? Forgiveness and healing were going to come slowly, that was clear, as I filtered out the legalistic demands of the CCOC from God's apparent grace so I could finally understand my true relationship with Him.

I had an educated guess about where I stood with God. I guessed that He was disappointed with me and probably a little pissed off. I felt like damaged goods, yet it appeared I had it all—especially once my lawyer notified me that my frivolous lawsuit was dropped. (It would later be refiled and dropped again.) It's funny how life can look so good on the outside while a war rages within.

One week later, I was reintroduced to my ABC's: *Adversity + Belief = Consequence*. This model demonstrates why a repeating pattern of old behavior occurs. For example, in my case, the adversity of my own sin added to my belief that God wanted to condemn me gave rise to the consequential emotion of anxiety and fear.

Now add D and E to the equation. *Adversity + Belief + Consequence + Disputed Belief = New Emotion*. When I dispute within my soul that God is not angry and condemning but is loving and forgiving, I will experience new, consequential emotions of peace, safety, security, and even joy.

That's great for others, but I couldn't see how I could ever be effective in disputing my own soul. I had taught other people about His saving love in home Bible studies and Sunday schools. I'd even taught it from the pulpit. I could teach it quite well, but I never fully bought what I was selling.

What a strange truth. It would be echoed to me seven years later by a Presbyterian pastor within an hour of meeting me. How is it possible to have so much Scripture within my mind but not within my heart?

I thought I knew what faith was. As the Scripture says, faith is "the substance of things hoped for, the evidence of things unseen." That's true, but Bryce helped me see that it is far more. Faith exists on a continuum between trust and doubt. When faith is closer to trust, we find hope. When faith is closer to doubt, we find despair. When doubt comes, we must reorder our thinking and take our thoughts captive for Christ so that we can move toward trust. The nature of faith excludes perfection, which presented a challenge to me. Bryce was trying to let me know that it is OK for my faith to be in process.

Last, we got off on a tangent about feeling guilty about my income, and even about being unhappy with what President Obama's policies might do to reduce it. I was living in a classic "damned-if-you-do/damned-if-you-don't" scenario. I couldn't be pleased. Being a wealthy surgeon bugged me. I felt like I didn't deserve it. My ridiculous income felt shameful, no matter how much I tithed and gave away to charity.

I loved what my counselor was doing for me, and I daydreamed about what it would be like to have a job like his. He seemed to be at peace, and I wanted that so badly. Bryce responded that we often want what others have on the outside, while having no idea what is truly going on inside. To address my financial identity struggle, he shared that God had gifted me with the ability to create wealth. I was to steward His money. By doing so, I created many more ministry opportunities than I would have as a minister or counselor.

Our weekly meetings were progressively uncovering issues that had been unconsciously, adversely affecting my life. I had come to bitterly hate the CCOC, but my parents were the face of that church. Transferring that emotion toward my parents caused me to resent them for what they subjected me to. I loved my parents. They needed me, and I wanted to be there for them without feeling angry and bitter. Light was shining on a lack of forgiveness in my heart, but my ruminating prayers to help me forgive were slow to be answered.

Bryce could see I needed help moving forward. He first pointed out what should have been obvious to me: My parents didn't realize what they were doing would hurt me. I needed to be like Jesus when He cried out on the cross, "Father, forgive them for they know not what they do."

The counselor then told me that my parents needed the intense religious structure the CCOC had to offer. God's grace gives us all the freedom to seek His Son in different ways. Their way involved rules, but I sought a relationship and freedom. The hurdle to my forgiveness was feeling like my parents needed to change. How could I forgive them for what their church did to me if they still loved that church? Bryce pointed out that I wanted to see repentance, which can be described as "turning to God for sanctification." But that is exactly what my parents had always done: turn to God. They lived a repentant life. With that realization, I could forgive them.

As I considered my relationship with my parents, one topic in particular stood out: church discipline. It was something discussed in the adult class at the CCOC nearly every year. As high school and college students, my brother and I, along with our girlfriends, had sat in that adult class twice a week. The discussions were often melancholy and cold.

I recall one couple had an "erring child" whom they had kicked out of the house for drug abuse after everything else failed. They called it "tough love," and given the circumstances, it seemed reasonable. However, the consensus of the adult class was that if the church disciplines a child for any reason whatsoever, then the parents should not even eat at the same dinner table with that unrepentant sinner.

I remember sitting there in my mint green Converse high tops, acid-washed blue jeans, and a black rock concert T-shirt, listening to how God wanted my parents to disassociate with me if I left the "one true church" in an effort to shame me and hasten my return. My dad always seemed conflicted about this, but my mom wasn't. She thought any parent would be nutty to shun their own kid.

All this self-examination was getting exhausting. When would I ever feel OK? Why did I feel like something was just not right? When would I become comfortable with grace? To those questions, Bryce responded with one of his own:

"If I were to offer you one million dollars with no strings attached, would you accept?"

"No," I replied.

"Why not?"

"I don't know. It doesn't seem right."

"Why not?"

"Because there has to be some kind of string attached."

"No, there's not. I told you there were none, and I meant it. You have no conditions to meet. You simply just take the money and walk away. Would you do it?"

"No. I don't believe you."

"David, don't you see it? You cannot accept gifts. You're probably the type of guy who always has to pick up the tab when you're at lunch with a friend."

Guilty as charged, I thought.

He continued. "You resist letting others bless you with a free meal just as much as you resisted my million bucks. How do you react when a patient expresses gratitude for what you've done?"

"I usually feel embarrassed, look away, and deflect the praise to my team and God," I said.

"Why don't you try looking the person in the eye and simply receive their gratitude?"

"I guess I don't feel like I deserve it."

"Kind of like you don't feel like you deserve God's grace?"

"Exactly."

Tears were streaming down my face at this point.

"None of us do," Bryce said. "That is why we need a Savior. You have to learn to accept God's grace freely, and then you'll feel the peace and joy you desire. Think about the joy in giving. You wouldn't have any joy if the gift wasn't received. Perhaps you need some spiritual disciplines as a way to bring healthy structure to your freedom in Christ. In doing what Jesus did, you will gradually learn to feel as accepted by the Father as Jesus did."

And with that charge, I left his office dumbfounded by how much mental and spiritual work lay before me. I prayed it would all be worth it one day.

It's OK to Be You

Our fifth meeting was a treasure trove of truth about God's purpose for my life. I had mentioned to Bryce that I had a nagging sense that I was supposed to be doing more. Maybe I was supposed to give up my practice for ministry and get a master's degree in divinity. Bryce asked if I thought I was a good surgeon. I had trouble answering, not because I didn't know the truth but because I struggled to say it out loud. I didn't want to sound proud.

Bryce explained that truth is neutral. Humility is knowing what you know and what you don't know. If you know you're a good surgeon, it is not bragging to say out loud that you are a good or even great surgeon. He thought my reluctance to claim it stemmed from my difficulty accepting gifts. Since God had gifted me with surgical talents, I needed to accept them and own who I am.

According to Bryce, this confusion over my calling kept me overly busy and confused about my purpose. To help, he pulled out his whiteboard and drew a Venn diagram with the words *best*, *purpose*, and *passion* written in the overlapping circles. I recognized it, and he appropriately cited it as coming from the book *Good to Great* by Jim Collins. He explained that what you can be the best at and have a passion for is a hobby. What you can be the best at and gain resources from is a job. What you have a passion for and resources for is a cause. The key is to discover what God has gifted you with that accomplishes all three. Whatever that is, it's your true calling: something you can be the best at, have a passion for, and gain resources from doing.

Bryce proposed that, as a poor receiver of gifts, I could not accept my purpose. As he put it, "when you accept your giftedness as a surgeon, then you can accept your purpose and rest in God's grace and stop scurrying around trying to do God's job by defining your own calling."

Finally, the counselor said I would only find rest from the weariness of pursuing my calling when I accepted God's calling, and God had clearly called me to be a great total joint surgeon who stewards His money for His purpose. Bryce said, "Just be His child, follow His lead, and stop trying to make your own way."

That was easier said than done. It felt awkward hearing him praise me as a surgeon, just as awkward as receiving my patients' gratitude. I thought I was being humble, but Bryce had revealed that I was actually quite arrogant. It shocked me to realize this. He said God had gifted me, and that if I wouldn't accept His gifts, I was placing myself above God and judging myself as not worthy of what God had given.

This goes back to what he said earlier about allowing the giver to experience joy in receiving the gift. For a young man whose life's theme was "you're not good enough," it was hard to accept that, in Him and through Him, I was good enough, and not only good enough, I was called to be a rich surgeon.

"The bottom line," he said, "is that it is OK to be you."

The tears streaming down my cheeks surprised me. Could all of it be true?

It all felt so fragile. Faith seemed fragile. It was easier to receive imposed convictions, which force you to think this and do that. Convictions felt comfortable. As long as I checked all the boxes on the list, I was supposed to be OK, but I wasn't. There were too many boxes. And anyway, all of these CCOC convictions belonged to someone else's faith. Now, I was discovering my own "measure of faith."

Finishing up the session, Bryce encouraged me that God wanted me to come to Him no matter what—in trust, in doubt, in fear, even in accusation.

"The problem isn't the negative emotions," he said. "It is not coming to God in faith with those negative emotions. Just like I want my kids to come to me, God wants me to come to Him. Satan's best weapon is making us feel too ashamed to go to the

Father. You must stop hiding, stop running, stop the frenetic busyness, and rest in His grace."

Overcoming the God of Fear

Since Christmas was drawing near, I had my next two sessions just weeks apart. On December 13, 2009, I opened up about a deeply rooted fear: that I would end up with dementia like my father and grandmother, and all my efforts at saving for the future would be for naught. The correct response was obvious. You have to live in the moment. The future will always be uncertain, so I was encouraged to practice the spiritual discipline of living life in balance.

But how was I supposed to do that with all the pressure I was under? I was afraid I needed surgery for my back pain, which made me even more fearful of missing work and potentially failing to find relief after surgery. And who would I choose to perform the surgery?

Fear kept rearing its ugly head in our conversations, and with Bryce's help, I came to realize I had been raised in a culture of fear. Fear was my normal. I was comfortable with it and quite uncomfortable without it. This revelation simultaneously rang as true as a tuning fork and as false as a politician. Why would anyone want to live in fear? The counselor explained that without fear, you have to trust God. Ultimately, I clung to fear so I wouldn't have to trust Him fully. When he said it, I sat there, stunned and speechless. I knew I wasn't good at trusting, and Bryce had figured it out.

He encouraged me to be thankful for pain as a God-given protector, to listen to it, to pray to God and listen for His reply, to take it slow, and, above all, to trust. That was a pretty tall order! Sensing my apprehension, he alluded to Romans 8:15 and told me to "live in the Spirit of sonship, not fear." He followed up by noting that Peter was fearful when he denied Jesus three times, but after the ascension, once the Holy Spirit dwelled within him, Peter lived a life of power, love, and trust. Peter wasn't perfect, but he was changed. Bryce pointed to Peter as an example of how God can bring change by His grace through His Spirit.

I then revealed another fear: celebrating Christmas together with my parents. Times were changing, and I didn't know how to feel about them. Bryce exposed the fact that I was actually afraid that what I was experiencing in grace wasn't real and that maybe the religious legalism happening a block and a half away at Mom and Dad's house was true.

Fear is such a deceiver. He pointed my attention to my wife, Sherry, a stable force of love and security in my life. I'd always had tremendous fear about my relationship with her, but once there were no more secrets between us, that fear went away. Before my confession, I had not fully received her love and instead often felt needy. Now I had trust in her love and a full assurance that it was unconditional. Giving up fear is possible. I had already done that with Sherry, so Bryce challenged me to be patient and let it happen with my family at Christmas.

The final counseling session that year occurred three days before Christmas. Feeling a bit spiritually dry and emotionally exhausted, I decided to spend a day at our lake house in prayer and contemplation. In the quiet of solitude, I felt God's embrace as He whispered, *Do not fear, for I am with you; do not be dismayed, for I am your God. I will strengthen you and help you; I will uphold you with my righteous right hand. For I am the Lord your God who takes hold of your right hand and says to you, Do not fear; I will help you.*

I returned home refreshed and rested until I shared the experience with my mother. We had a conflict over God's grace, and all of a sudden, I was hit with the full measure of fear and doubt again. The feeling was so frustrating. I just wanted to feel the "peace that surpasses all understanding."

I later asked Bryce, "Why does the fear come rushing back like that?"

We went through some "if, then" scenarios, which is a great way to get to the bottom of your feelings. If Mom is mad, then I am bad. If I am bad, then I need to repent and be good. If I don't, then something is wrong with me. That kind of thinking created pressure to right every wrong, and with that pressure came the fear of not being right in my newfound grace. God's grace seemed way too easy, too unjust.

I couldn't quite wrap my mind around the fact that when Jesus cried from the cross, "It is finished," it truly was finished. He did what I could not. He paid the price that was demanded of me. I deserved death, but He gave me life. With that gospel truth, I realized that it is not my responsibility to make all things right. I am not the Savior; Jesus is. The faulty moral compass that said, "If I don't line up with the CCOC, then I am damned to hell," had to be crushed under the weight of the gospel.

Bryce shared a similar experience he'd had with his legalistic mother. He finally asked her if she thought he was stupid. Then he asked her to respect him as an intelligent person capable of drawing his own conclusions, rather than borrowing hers. Finally, they reached a point where they could call each other out on their manipulative behavior and still love each other.

Evidently, it all started with him having a beer in front of his mom. With that one beer, Pandora's box was opened.

Bryce and I talked about Jesus turning water into wine and Paul telling Timothy to have an anxiolytic glass of wine. As corny as it sounds, Bryce confessed that he would occasionally raise a glass of wine to Jesus in gratitude for His freedom. That was way too much for me. I vomited up all my fears of drinking, of being a poor example to my kids, of being judged as unfit to become a church elder.

His reply was crushing. "David, your god is fear," he said. "You need to lie at the feet of Jesus and accept His grace and realize once and for all that He did not give us a Spirit of fear but of sonship!"

With tears falling yet again, our time was up, and he encouraged me to relax, love my dysfunctional family, and enjoy Jesus this Christmas.

Cairn stones of confession, grace, and healing marked 2009 as a beautiful milestone on my journey of faith. God's presence never felt more real than when He gave me the humility to confess and find healing in counseling. The wisdom I gained from Bryce Roland pointed me forward on a path of trusting in God as my steadfast, loving Father. I began to see the truth that He loves me as I am.

As I devoured books like Brennan Manning's *The Ragamuffin Gospel* and Sam Storm's *Singing God*, I realized that the flickering flame of my faith would need some kindling and air before it would become a bonfire of trust. From Donald Miller's book *Blue Like Jazz*, it became obvious to me that I had to completely accept my Father God's love lest I remain an insecure, needy, self-loathing boy, who not only could not accept God's love, but anyone else's love for that matter—including Sherry's.

The journey would only become more difficult in later years, but at least then I had hope that I was headed in the right direction.

Chapter 19

QUESTIONING THE CALL

Reality

He makes my reality
I am a living virtuosity
By Christ set free
I am not me
But Christ
Alive in me
He takes my frustration
Restlessness and damnation
He erases the pain
Removes the stain
By His blood
I am washed clean
I am free to be me
He lifts me out
Of my self-destructive pit
With His love

My heart's darkness is lit
He shines to me
In me, and through me
The good you see
Is Christ in me
By Christ set free
I am not me
But Christ alive
In me

I WAS EXCITED TO have caught the vision of Christ's grace and freedom, so naturally I wanted to share it with others. Sometimes I yearned to share it so much that I wondered if I was being called to do it full-time. Bryce and I had already discussed that issue twice, but it remained unresolved. Of course, a big career change like that made no sense. It seemed ridiculous to spend fourteen years training in surgery only to practice it for a few years. That was absurd both financially and intellectually. Nevertheless, my racing mind often ruminated on what it would be like to go into ministry and share the good news of grace as a full-time calling.

A patient that I will forever refer to as "my angel" appeared in my clinic a couple of weeks into 2010. She was four months out from a bilateral total knee procedure, which I'd felt compelled to do even though she had too many risk factors for complications after such an extensive surgery. However, by her report and my observation, she had escaped harm and experienced a beautiful outcome. So naturally, we spent our clinic time on more important matters.

First, she told me she'd felt torn between another surgeon and me, but God had directed her to me. She also told me that God had often prompted her to pray for me ever since we'd met. She didn't necessarily know why, but she was always faithful to pray for me. When she said this, the love in her eyes drew me to her, and I confessed that I wasn't sure what God wanted from me. Without hesitation, she affirmed that God was using me to take sidelined, arthritic Christians and put them back on the front lines to fight the good fight of faith for Jesus.

My angel had once been active in ministry but had slowed down due to knee pain. Now, as a result of the successful surgery, she was back in ministry and full speed ahead. She encouraged me to keep doing the same for others. Then she prayed for me right there in the clinic.

Finally, as I walked out the door, she said, "Keep shining for Jesus." I don't think it's a coincidence that those are the very words I used when sending my kids to school in the morning.

Adoption and Agony

As others continued to affirm my calling, my spiritual life finally began to make sense. One of the most significant affirmations came in the form of a request. A couple who had been our best friends during residency lived in a big midwestern city and were friends with a socialite named Charity. Charity had become pregnant from an adulterous affair. Not wanting to wear a scarlet letter *A*, she was considering an abortion. It seemed like her only solution to maintain status.

Ultimately, Charity decided to keep the baby and give her up for private placement adoption, but only if she could find a loving, wealthy, educated couple to raise the baby. Though we were not much for social climbing, Sherry and I fit the bill since we met her three qualifiers. Our friends approached us and presented the opportunity. At the time, I had desperately wanted a fourth child, but perinatal nausea and vomiting had prevented it. This seemed like our chance.

Sherry and I prayed, pondered, and discussed adoption for a week or two. We had limited time to decide since the mother intended to abort her child if she could find no other way out of this self-inflicted burden of being perfect. The more we prayed about it, the more Sherry and I began to feel excited about the prospect of having another baby girl.

Finally, we decided it was time to talk to the kids about it. Explaining to a ten-year-old girl and her twelve- and fourteen-year-old brothers that they were about to have a newborn sister required a fine balance between motivation and manipulation, fantasy and reality, status quo and seismic change. However, as best we could tell, they were all on board.

In the midst of this joyful anticipation of expanding our family, I began to doubt whether I could handle the physical demands of parenting a newborn. My herniated lumbar L5-S1 disk gave me constant buttock and leg pain, and lately, numbness. When I noticed I was having trouble going up the stairs because of weakness, I decided it was time for surgery. I had eight years of working with intermittent pain, partially alleviated by fifteen epidural steroid injections and physical therapy, and now I was numb and weak and facing permanent nerve damage.

Finally, on February 2, 2010, I had an outpatient microdiscectomy, which gave me instant relief from the leg pain, numbness, and weakness. It seemed like a perfect success. A month later, I was doing great and back to work. In fact, I felt so good that I went to retrieve our boat from storage. This would be our last summer with just the three kids to enjoy. By fall, we'd have four, so I wanted to make the most of it! This was also my first winter with a boat in storage, and unfortunately, I'd forgotten to put the battery on a trickle charger. When I realized the battery was dead, I bent forward (a bad idea) and reached out to lift it (a worse idea). The battery wouldn't budge, so in a fit of exhaustion and anger, I jerked it as hard as I could toward me (worst idea). I got the battery out, along with the rest of my L5-S1 disk and a portion of my C6-7 cervical disk.

The pain was so intense, I couldn't even look up. My head and eyes were forced into a downward gaze to keep the electrical shock from penetrating my neck and right arm. My butt cheek was on fire. I had no choice but to finish in pain. I drove the boat on its trailer to the lake house, dropped it off, and returned home. I hated having to report my stupidity to Sherry, who had wisely cautioned me earlier not to overdo it.

By the time I got back home, I could tell that I was in big trouble. My right triceps felt weak, and my middle finger was numb. I had to keep my head tilted to the left and down to prevent the shooting electrical, ten-out-of-ten pain. I went straight to the interventional radiologist for a cervical epidural steroid injection. Afterward, I could look straight ahead but not up, not until a second shot a few days later. Overall, it took a month, but by God's grace and answered prayer, the neck pain, arm weakness, and hand numbness gradually improved.

Devastating News

My back continued to agonize me, but I was on a mission like never before. After conceiving, coordinating, funding, and preaching a men's conference at the Garth Street church called "Men's FITness" (fear, identity, and trust), I received one affirmation after another. Most importantly, my brother came from Kansas City to be consoled about problems in his life. We bonded as he opened up to me for the first time that I can ever recall.

After attending the conference, he described it as a "turning point" in his life. I was stunned when an old med school friend from Adams City used those same words. Around that time, a nurse anesthetist told me that people at work saw Jesus in me. My partner Phil said he saw the Holy Spirit working in me. An old CCOC buddy said he saw Christ in me. My nurse practitioner said she had seen a change in me. With all of this affirmation, it was clear that God was using me for His purpose, and I wanted more.

Surely, it seemed, He wanted me to give my life to serving Him through counseling ministry, helping others with the help I had received. I wanted to do more. I felt His favor, and I wanted to earn more of it. More than ever, my thoughts were clouded with doubt over whether to continue as a surgeon or leave it all behind and go to seminary. I thought, *That would be quite an awesome story. What a great impact I could have!*

And then we got the devastating news: Charity aborted her baby.

The news came in a phone call on a Saturday during Spencer's competitive league basketball tournament. Horrified and sad, Sherry and I left the gym to walk the outdoor track while Alex and Paige followed along. We weren't sure how to break the news to the other kids. Would they see our grief and feel like they were not enough? Would they feel the same grief? Everyone had been feeling so excited about welcoming the baby. How could we tell them it wasn't going to happen? With each circuit around the track, the grief felt heavier. The burden was crushing.

Finally, after the last game, we walked the track with all three kids and shared the painful news. It stopped us in our tracks as we held each other and cried.

I couldn't make sense of it. What was God trying to teach us? All I felt was loss without purpose. I could find no good in this situation. I ruminated about having a vasectomy reversal and trying again, but Sherry rejected the notion of being pregnant again. We felt lost. The song "I'll Worship While I'm Waiting" came on the radio and brought some comfort, but we were lost in grief.

In the meantime, my back and butt pain became unbearable, and I reluctantly agreed to have a repeat microdiscectomy and anterior interbody fusion. My first surgeon was a close friend. However, I was afraid of having a bad outcome, so I moved to a different surgeon who had more experience in ALIFs. He brought on a neurosurgeon to peel the scar from my entrapped nerve and an accomplished general vascular surgeon to open up the belly down to the spine. I now had a team of experts on my side, but I felt like I had betrayed my friend by not involving him in a procedure that might turn out to be a disaster.

Despite my best efforts at controlling the outcome, I had a worse-than-typical surgical experience. Opioids brought little pain relief and an abundance of nausea. Because of my previous Lap Nissen, I could no longer vomit, so I just wretched. I lost three days in a sea of opioid-induced agony that was unlike anything I'd experienced in all my past surgeries or episodes of stomach flu combined. Yet I clung to a small lifeline of hope because my butt pain and leg numbness were gone. If I could survive the surgical pain and post-op nausea, the surgery would be a success—and I did, and it was.

Keeping Everyone Happy

Sadly, tragedy continued to hit. A few weeks after my surgery, my partner Phil died jumping hills with the top down in his BMW M series convertible. The year had become one tragedy after another. This one hit too close to home. Our youngest daughter and his youngest daughter were close friends who attended the same private Christian school. His two older daughters were the same age as our older sons. Something just clicked between us as our lives became almost inseparable that summer.

Later, Phil's wife, Gretchen, told us that we "suspended" her through the mourning of Phil's death. However, she knew that she and her girls needed to be close to her family in Wyoming, so just as quickly as they entered our lives, they left.

That summer, I really needed to talk to my counselor, Bryce. While everything else was going on around me, I was knee deep in a master's level Old Testament survey class. I was just dipping my toes into the waters of seminary, but I knew I wouldn't have enough time to return to work and complete the class. I was more convinced that God wanted me to be a surgeon and intended to use me as a minister in that role. Honestly, I wasn't really sure why I'd gone back to school.

I brought Bryce up to date on everything that had been happening and shared my concern about returning to work and the likelihood of overdoing it to keep everyone happy. Then we talked about my taking a seminary course. Bryce said, "There's a difference between getting an education and earning a degree." He encouraged me to stay in the class to grow in my faith, because it would help me fulfill God's calling to teach and counsel patients and friends. However, he cautioned me not to get "puffed up with knowledge," since I'd already been a victim of that kind of religious arrogance.

"You are an instrument in the hands of the Redeemer," Bryce said. "And God can redeem everything you learned in your CCOC upbringing and use it for His glory."

As far as feeling conflicted, Bryce said, "David, you have an easy time taking care of everyone else but not such an easy time taking care of David."

He encouraged me not to be in such a rush to return to work. I had such high expectations about returning that I was likely to be disappointed. "You need to prioritize taking care of yourself," he said.

He went on to explain that my identity needed to be in Christ, not in the approval of coworkers or patients. If I had to cancel a case and limit myself to two or three, then so be it. I would be setting a good example for my patients about not overdoing it.

Bryce was equally concerned about my marriage. Sherry was getting busier as an interior decorator, which meant she was often unavailable. When present, she was usually distracted. Bryce concluded our meeting by offering me some advice on conflict resolution.

The Fog of Shame Begins to Lift

Adjusting to life back at work went about like I expected, difficult but manageable. The stress brought on more neck pain, which was mostly alleviated by several facet joint injections. I decided it was time to lighten my load. I served on the board of a title insurance company in which I had invested, as well as the board of my homeowners' association. I quit both. I also convinced the seminary to let me withdraw from class with an "incomplete" instead of dropping out with an F. Typical of me, I was trying to control the outcome as best I could.

Soon enough, however, the uncontrollable smacked me back down to the pavement like Dicky Packer did after my third-grade piano lesson. I had been using metal-on-metal hip replacements to reduce polyethylene wear. A special implant from Depuy called the ASR (articulating surface replacement) seemed beneficial in about thirty of my highly active patients. When studies began to show failures, and researchers complained that the company was not addressing their concerns, I quit using the ASR. A year later, a recall was issued for all ASR implants.

It was astonishing to me. How can something like this happen in modern American medicine? The FDA agreed that the company had improved metal-on-metal technology enough to approve its use, and I bought into their confidence with a false sense of security. Later, I learned that the FDA's 510(k) approval was based solely on the fact that they had already approved something sufficiently similar in the past. I felt foolish and manipulated. I'd put these faulty implants in thirty of my patients!

I was at my wit's end. Fearing the harm to my patients and the possibility of a barrage of lawsuits, I sent letters to all thirty patients and began seeing them back in the clinic to monitor their progress. (Eventually, years later, I ended up re-operating on nearly all of those patients.) But the extreme stress meant I had to see Bryce again.

Just before Thanksgiving, we met and talked about work stress, and I learned from him that the solution was to learn to live within my circle of responsibility. I tend to make the circle way bigger than it is. I feel like I have to be the perfect father, husband, surgeon, and Christian. That's the circle I see, but God's circle for me is much smaller. Concerning the ASR recall, Bryce affirmed that I had done my best with the information I had at the time, so I had no reason to feel guilty. I just needed to learn and grow.

If I were perfect, what would be the point of learning, growing, or doing anything? So instead of striving for perfection and thinking the same old thoughts, believing the old lies, stressing, and worrying, I just had to learn the joy of being adequate, even if barely.

I kept thinking I should do more, be more. I couldn't seem to stop playing the old tapes and wrong beliefs in my head. They were still ruling my thinking, actions, and emotions. They were also causing intermittent chest pains and a pervading sense of being overwhelmed.

"I feel like I should go to Haiti on a mission trip," I told Bryce. "Or like I should be able to care for all who seek my help. I just feel like I should be able to make everyone happy."

He replied that *should* is a danger sign. When you hear *should*, you need to ask, *Why?* When I feel I should do something, is it because I have to prove something, prove my worth, my devotion, my love? Basically, he said, "Don't should on yourself."

Covered in "should," I simply felt afraid and ashamed. I couldn't see myself as a reliable role model for my daughter, Paige, in choosing a husband. I could pray that the boys would find someone like Sherry, but no way could I pray the same for Paige about me. Bryce told me the root cause of this disparity in how I see myself versus how God sees me is nothing more than shame—unhelpful, deceitful self-condemnation that I hadn't let go of. Finally, correcting my self-analysis, he said, "David, you are a man of integrity."

At the conclusion of the session, he opened the door to some healthier ways of coping with stress. In addition to alpha wave stimulation, which I'd never tried, he talked about how to meditate. He explained that he preps the room, closes his eyes, and pictures a walk in the forest. He imagines all the sensory experiences—moist air, the sound of crickets, the sight of the leaves, tree bark, animals, and so on. Then, he sits on a log and imagines Jesus sitting beside him. They sit quietly, and finally, he asks Jesus if He has something to say. He may or may not, but either way, his soul is refreshed.

Deer camp gave me quite a bit of time to process everything that Bryce had said. The shame that covered me was like a dense fog, and the only way to come out of the fog was to move on and get away from it. One thing was certain: It wasn't going to lift on its own. So I prayed and meditated. That year, rather than hunting in the morning, I went to worship and took communion. During the Lord's Supper, as I envisioned Christ on the cross, it felt as if Jesus came down from the cross to embrace me. His touch was palpable, and His effort to move me out of shame was surreal.

I shared this with a fellow CCOC survivor the next Sunday during the class I taught. She and I commiserated about how difficult it is to know your own identity in Christ when you've been brainwashed for so long. My wife and I eventually paid for her and her husband to have extensive counseling with Bryce. Both were as "wowed" by him as I was, but we all still had miles to go before we would ever truly believe that Romans 8:1 referred to us: "There is therefore now no condemnation for those who are in Christ Jesus" (Romans 8:1).

Chapter 20

AN ANXIOUS DIAGNOSIS HUMBLES AND HELPS

A Father's Walk with Jesus

I walked beside my Lord today
And listened as He spoke.
He told me that I slipped again
and failed to show His love.

He was in my home yesterday
And saw me lose control.
He said He was disappointed
In the harsh words I chose.

I told Him of my frustration,
I told Him that I cared,
I told Him I am conflicted
By the anger that I feel.

195

He said He's always in my heart
and knows the place He holds.
He knows I dearly love Him.
He knows how hard I try.

Suddenly I stopped to ask Him,
Why do you let me fail?
I want to give them grace,
But shame is what they feel.

Tears filled His eyes with compassion,
For He knows how much I love them.
He said His grace is sufficient
To make them feel secure.

Then He said let's just keep walking,
For when I am by your side,
They'll see My love and devotion
And know how hard you've tried.

They'll feel unconditional love.
They'll forgive as You have,
And they'll know they have a Savior
To always walk beside.

RELATIONSHIPS CAN BE a source of profound communal joy, but the relationships in my life seemed more like question marks at the end of what-ifs. Sherry was extraordinarily busy. What if she was doing this to get away from me, to make her own money in case she left me, to find someone else? What if I wasn't enough for her?

Winter's seasonal depression had been darker than usual. My mind was under assault on every front. Worry and fear were taking control of my thought life. No matter how hard I tried to control my thoughts, it was clear I was failing to cope.

Our ten-, twelve-, and fourteen-year-olds raised even more questions in my mind. What if they always fought and never learned to love each other? What if they got caught up in drugs and illicit sex? What if my example of drinking alcohol led one, two, or all three of them to become alcoholics? What if they brought partners or spouses into the family who were a bad fit? What if they failed? What if all this meant I had failed?

My parents presented uncertainty as well. What if I didn't visit them enough? What if I had to take on more of the full-time care of my dad? What if his continuing health decline from Parkinson's disease with Lewy body dementia became uncontrollable? Would I be a good enough son to my mom when she was a widow? What if I never got past seeing them as the faces of CCOC?

Wherever I went, I could not escape my anxious fears. My mind constantly raced with questions about fears that seemed to come as often as breathing, and I personalized everything. At work, I was busy with a 10 percent increase in surgical volume. Keeping up seemed impossible. Did all the patients who waited more than ten minutes hate me, or did it take thirty or sixty minutes to hate? When a patient experienced a complication, how much did they blame and hate their physician? Was my chest pain ever going to stop? Would my left-hand ring finger and little finger Raynaud's continue to activate during high levels of job stress? Was my body going to hold up? How many more surgeries would I have to have? Was the neck pain just stress, or was it the result of cervical degenerative changes?

Drowning in a sea of anxiety, I looked for private help first. *The Anxiety and Worry Workbook: The Cognitive Behavioral Solution* by Clark and Beck proved useful in explaining anxiety and its root in fear. The book helped me enumerate my anxious concerns along with the emotions and destructive thinking associated with them. It also provided a new way of thinking. Helpful as it was, I wasn't ready to relinquish control, so my anxiety levels continued to rise. I turned to religion to keep my head above water.

Drawing Near to the Throne of Grace

Much of my quiet time in the spring of 2011 was spent in meditation and reflection on God and His love for us. Communion on Sundays often brought peaceful encounters with Jesus, who encouraged me with thoughts of peace. At times, it even seemed as if His arms were embracing me as He whispered, "Rest in Me, David." I didn't know if it was really Him or just my own thoughts, but either way, it felt good for a fleeting moment.

However, the fears always returned eventually, like excited teenagers on the last day of school, ready to wreak havoc. Work stress had me cycling through burnout regularly, yet it also afforded opportunity for renewal. Patients with whom I could make a spiritual connection often sustained me. Whether through a discussion of theology or a simple prayer, many patients gave me the strength to finish the day. One particular day in clinic, my "angel" admonished me to "rejoice in fiery trials." She then took my hands and prayed a blessing over me, reminding me of who I am in Christ. How many surgeons get that?

Even so, I could not rest, could not find peace, could not stop the racing anxious thoughts. They made me a monster at times.

Explosive and volatile, I was nothing like the man I wanted to be. I felt helpless, desperate to find some relief, not just for me, but for my family. What husband wants to hear his wife say, "David, if only I had a recording of your outburst, then you'd see how foolish and shameful you just behaved?" I had to do something. I was almost forty years old and starting to think I suffered from chronic mental illness.

Convinced that kava kava might be the solution, I began researching natural remedies because I knew I could take them without having to confide in a healthcare professional that I suffered from anxiety. Letting someone know seemed too risky for my job security. What if my referring doctors lost confidence in me when they found out about my anxiety? Would they stop sending me patients? What would my partners think or do? What if I lost my license? Yes, kava kava seemed like my best option, despite the FDA's hands-off approach to supplements, which meant I would never truly know what ingredients were in any bottle labeled "kava kava." It didn't matter anyway, because, as it turned out, it didn't help.

On our ski trip in Utah, we went to church and heard a sermon on cognitive distortions and how to turn those false beliefs over to God. I had been struggling with the fear of having generalized anxiety disorder and having to take psych meds, and God decided to enlighten my psychological understanding through a perfectly timed sermon. Mind-reading, all-or-nothing, and future predicting were just some of the struggles mentioned. I wondered if learning more about this topic would help me avoid being diagnosed with a mental illness and put on psych meds for the rest of my life.

Eventually, I found an incredibly helpful book called *SOS Help for the Emotions: Managing Anxiety, Anger, and Depression* by Lynn Clark. Thinking about my thoughts through the lens of rational emotive behavioral therapy was helpful but proved an incomplete fix.

Still, that morning at church, I had poured out my anguish to God over my anxiety, and God seemed to show up magnificently. The sermon convinced me that I needed more help than just recognizing my cognitive distortions, but I feared that meant taking medication. My biggest concern was that anxiety and perfectionism were what made me such a talented surgeon. If I took medication that helped me relax, would I become sloppy? Would my typical good outcome change? It didn't console me that nothing like that had happened when I took medicine for depression. Reason doesn't have an audible voice in an anxious mind.

In that moment, God took control and whispered, "I love you, David," to which I quickly replied, "I'm scared."

God assured me, "It's OK. I am with you. I will help you."

I pleaded with Him, "I don't want to feel uneasy and sad all the time. I just want to feel joy."

God's presence lingered with me, as He replied, "My grace is sufficient for you; I will never leave or forsake you."

And that was it. A surreal moment. Had God really just conversed with me, or was it all me? I decided it was best not to question it and simply embrace it. Somehow God was going to make a way.

God's Grace Plus Medication

God kept showing up in personal ways I'd never experienced before. One day in June, while reading Colossians 1–3 and praying at home, I begged God for relief from the burden of so many anxious thoughts about Sherry's work and the kids' bickering (and my overreacting to both). God brought to mind a deep truth. He revealed that my anxiety stemmed from a desire for control and a lack of trust in God.

Another day, while sitting on a bench at a local hiking trail, where I often sat to pray for my dad, I heard God say, "I AM the living water, I AM the way, I AM the truth, I AM the life. I AM the vine." Then, on my fortieth birthday, while walking the trail and thinking about how redundant life seemed, God reminded me that every step may look the same, but with each one, I was getting closer to Him for eternity.

While visiting a church during summer vacation in South Carolina, God convicted me to repent of my anger and volatility. The pastor offered everyone the opportunity to write down their struggles on a piece of paper and nail it to the cross. I approached the cross with my little piece of paper, determined to do better, and returned to my family confessing the same.

On our second summer vacation to Hawaii, while celebrating Sherry's fortieth, I was overwhelmed by God's presence and love, a feeling that competed with the anxiety I often felt during travel. Struggling to enjoy Hawaii was certainly a clue that I needed more help.

Despite these powerful spiritual moments, my mind—and resulting behavior—were still such a wreck that during one of many fights with Sherry, she asked me to go ahead and cheat and get it over with. She was convinced that in my unhappiness, I would be unfaithful—just like her father had been to her mother, just like Darius, just like so many other professional men that we knew.

I had been to see Bryce that summer for some marital counseling, but I still wasn't loving my wife well. It was humbling to realize this, but I had to find a way to do better and to make her feel more secure. I finally made an appointment with Dr.

Shauder at the end of August, and he started me on Lexapro. He also encouraged me to adopt a more positive outlook on life, especially as it related to Sherry. He reminded me that she was a terrific wife who had supported me during my training, taken care of our children at home when they were young, and was also a beautiful, gifted artist who deserved her time to shine. Dr. Shauder was right.

And so my medication odyssey began. I started with Lexapro at twenty milligrams daily. In a month, I was doing much better mentally, but I lost the ability to ejaculate, which put me back in the doctor's office pretty quickly. I went off Lexapro and tried some samples of Vibryd. A tidal wave of chest pain and anxiety swept me back into the doctor's office a third time, for what I feared would be strike three. However, Shauder put me back on Lexapro, reduced to ten milligrams per day, along with some Xanax at 0.25 milligrams for the chest pain episodes that occurred outside of the OR. That exception was easy because the OR was where I felt emotionally at my best, likely because of my sense of control. Finally, my mind slowed to a tolerable pace, and I became a better person to be around.

Lexapro was good for the mind but did little for my heart. I remained angry and bitter with Sherry for leaving the home to start a career. Everything around the house that was left undone seemed like a sign of her rejection (at least, that is how I misinterpreted it). If I asked her about any of it, we always wound up fighting. From my point of view, I was certainly not going to clean, do the dishes, and go to the grocery store after working hard all day. In my stubborn pride, I refused to take any ownership of my share of the household responsibilities. When I asked her to hire someone to do laundry or cook, we fought more.

We took a brief time-out from fighting for me to have right-shoulder surgery. However, once I healed and returned to work, our relationship continued to decline. We desperately needed to get away and renew our vows.

As it happened, a national Christian youth organization invited us to a Donor's Weekend in November in Boca Raton. The timing was perfect. That weekend introduced us to new friends, incredible food, inspiring times of worship, and convicting lessons.

We were refreshed spiritually, but I was sexually frustrated on Lexapro. My doctor had given me a Viagra sample to see if it hastened my climax. I took it and turned our hotel suite into a dark comedy skit. Blood was everywhere, yet I couldn't find the source anywhere. Was it me or Sherry? I ran to the toilet, leaving behind a trail of blood. It was me. Sherry was terrified, and I was baffled. Was I cut? Was I bleeding from my anus? But why would I be bleeding from my anus? Did I have cancer? Was the blood coming out of my penis? Oh, God, would I have to go to the ER?

Finally, I saw it: A small scrotal hemangioma had burst. The blood vessel was the size of a pinhead but bled like a firehose. I had to hold pressure on it for an hour. My wife and I laughed ourselves silly as we replayed the ridiculous scene over and over. Finally, the bleeding stopped, and the conference went on.

The organization that coordinated the weekend retreat aimed to secure major commitments to meet expansion goals. Our kids had been to the organization's events and experienced spiritual highs. They were learning the importance of God's calling for His people to put their faith into action. So, the donors' weekend played upon our sympathies with stories that had us in tears. When it came to donating, we wondered what number was big enough to make a sacrifice? My wife and I prayed, discussed, and fought about what to give.

Ultimately, we separately decided to pledge $100,000, a gift we completed within a year. It certainly stretched us at times, especially with our weekly tithe and monthly Old Albatross $7,500 mortgage payment. I worried that this was just another attempt at earning God's and man's approval while soothing my guilty conscience for having so much wealth. Even so, our hearts were in the right place. We were trying to please God and give sacrificially to a cause that we felt was important.

Afraid of Sherry

By year's end, my anxiety was again off the charts. Medication was failing me. I decided to try more counseling. I didn't know it would be my last session with Bryce as he was moving to Colorado. We started by discussing my stressors, which were many: a scary global economy, increased government regulation on healthcare, an uncertain financial future in healthcare, a need to possibly hire someone else in the midst of a double-dip recession, switching men's groups, and finally (after some prodding) the unresolved conflict with Sherry over her career. I explained to Bryce that Sherry didn't respect my business advice and that her business was taking her away from home too much. To make matters worse, I feared that her expanding local market booth would become a tax burden come next April.

In all of these stressors, the underlying theme was loneliness. The counselor pointed out that God created us to be in close communion with our spouse and that I was lonely because Sherry was absent from my life in the stressful areas. We were beginning to live separate, parallel lives. I had given up on weekly lunch dates and struggled to get time for an occasional lunch or afternoon walk. All we had time for was work and kids, which left no time for us. Our lives rarely connected with romance or passion, but when they did, we both agreed—it was still amazing.

Bryce said we needed to date and try to rekindle the passion for each other because it would draw us closer, make us feel secure, and help us overcome our loneliness. However, to do so, we had to resolve the wedge that had been driven between us. That seemed like a monumental effort. Bryce likened me to King Saul and the Israelites when they were afraid of Goliath. As he put it, "If you know you are God's son, then you should know how to face your giants."

He said flat out that I was afraid of Sherry. That was true, and I knew it. She rarely listened to constructive criticism without defensiveness. She was ready to throw down at a moment's notice to get her way (e.g., extravagant Christmas parties in our home). Bryce revealed that I was too afraid to be honest with her about the pink elephant in the room (i.e., her work). Until that was cleared up, he said we would always feel distant, no matter how hard we tried to connect. Though I had tried to make peace, the unresolved conflict remained a deep wedge between us. The result was more loneliness, manifesting itself as anger and anxiety.

Finally, after once again confronting my too-high expectations in life, Bryce concluded with some alarming encouragement. He wanted me to undergo intensive group counseling to unlock my full potential in life. He saw me as a charismatic man with enough potential to be a change agent in the world. Bryce said some men are meant to be giants, and he believed I was one of them.

I was simultaneously flattered and dumbfounded, encouraged and defeated, hopeful and anxious. The notion was simply too much, but it lingered in my mind.

Chapter 21

FLOUNDERING

Last Days with Dad

At your bedside
Waiting for open eyes
Hoping for a smile

So little time left
I crawl into bed
I hold you like my child

The smell of your T-shirt
The familiar scent of my father
The ache in my heart grows

How much longer
Are you in pain
Can you hear me

What do you see
Angel choirs and Jesus enthroned
Or darkness, suffering, and longing

What do you feel
Hope and eternity
Or sadness and death

I sing hymns
Read favorite Scripture
Profess my love and gratitude

Will it be tonight
Will you awaken one last time
To say I love you, goodbye

Seven days without food
Seven days of palliative care
Seven days of quietness

I kiss your forehead
I hug your arms and chest
I even bathe you

I force your eyes open to see them one more time
Caribbean blue and beautiful
But with a frightening blank stare

This is real!

Dementia is giving way to death
No more bright smiles
When I enter the room
No more weakened efforts to arise
To give me a hug

A month ago
You stopped talking as much
Two weeks ago
You stopped walking
Last week
You stopped swallowing

Mom has cared for you to the end

Oh that the end
Was not so near

Tonight you are breathing so quickly
More morphine
More Ativan
More watching, waiting
Sleeplessly anticipating

I need sleep
Lying down I listen
To hear you breathe
I cannot sleep

Then it stops!

I race to your side
My brother gets our mom
We listen to you gasp for air
We wait for you to breathe again
Two more gasps
With my ear to your chest
Your heart slows
And then stops
It is finished

Pulseless and cool to touch
Your eyes do not react to light
Your eyes move like a doll's
I am your physician
I pronounce your death
Time of death 22:56

Two days later
At your funeral
I am your son again
Broken and hurt
Sobbing, grieving
I cannot let go
The pain is too much
The aching empty void is so vast

Our Father in heaven
Welcomes you
How long until I see you again
Will you visit me in my dreams
Will time move on
Until the day comes

When I miss thinking of you
I miss you
I rejoice at the thought
Of Jesus's embrace
But I miss you so much

IF YOU'VE EVER been fishing at the edge of a lake or pond, you've likely unhooked a fish only to have it fall to the grass. You may get finned when you pick the fish up to toss it back in the water, but the fish is obviously more disgruntled as it flops around, violently contracting its body in an effort to survive, return to water, and breathe again. Flipping from one side to the other, back and forth, somehow the fish gets closer to the water until you finally catch it again with your foot or hand. Or else it makes its way back to its natural habitat. Allegorically, for the next several years, I was the fish stuck on the shore, floundering but never making progress.

The constant barrage of onerous new healthcare regulations, daily concern for my dying father, endless efforts to do something big for God, the deepening divide in my marriage, along with the increasing evidence that I was failing as a parent, had my thought life spinning. No antidepressant could rein in the constant mental machinations. I felt no peace. A new counselor tried to help me with the Serenity Prayer, but I was stuck, lacking the wisdom to know what I could and could not control. I continued my moderate but more regular effort to escape the turmoil through alcohol. I wasn't drinking to extremes, just enough to get a helpful buzz, but this habit only served to increase my shame. I subconsciously heaped piles of guilt upon myself for acting contrary to the way I was raised. Eventually, my efforts to keep up with work, my wife, my kids, and my parents led to a worsening burnout.

Before spring break, my father became ill. I didn't know if it was another typical setback or if he was approaching the end. Either way, burnout was consuming me, and I had to get away. Spring Break typically meant a family trip to the beach, but we had decided earlier in the year to go skiing in Utah since we had skipped our usual Christmas break trip to Deer Valley. My brother committed to taking some time off from work to help us out with Dad so my family could go on our trip. With his presence, I felt comfortable enough to leave.

The last coherent words my dad ever spoke to me were right before I left his bedside to go blow off some steam on Powder Mountain. His words were, "Stay upright." With that bit of wisdom and a fifth of Glenfiddich fifteen-year-old Solera Reserve, we headed to the mountains.

The trip was most certainly a mixed blessing. On the one hand, I was able to forget about the stresses of my practice as I slalomed down the slopes, but on the other hand, I was constantly reminded of my dad as I answered repeated phone calls from my mom. Dad stopped eating and had to be hospitalized. Again, I wondered if this was it or if it would be like the other times when he bounced back.

After three days of skiing (and finishing my bottle of scotch), we flew back early to find Dad nonconversant and anorexic. He was already gaunt, but he would become much worse. Two weeks of sitting at his bedside in the hospital made it clear that this was indeed the end. And my dumb ass had been skiing in Utah! I felt such guilt. My mother consoled me that she would not have had it any other way. She reminded me that I had already been there for Dad through so much. We took him home for hospice care. He lived through the first night and passed away the next.

During those last two weeks, I read the Bible to him, prayed with him, sang hymns, and bathed him. I was there for him, for me, for Mom, and for Dan, too. The funeral was a catharsis of emotion: regret, anger, grief, sadness, burnout, and continued turmoil with my wife. I was crushed, undone, not knowing who came and went as I publicly released all that was pent up inside me. It was nonstop ugly crying for hours.

Then the funeral was over, and the grieving process continued. That was ugly too. I couldn't make sense of why God, in His "goodness and love," didn't let my parents have a nice retirement in their golden years. God took my father's health right at his retirement and then took his life six years later. Still, having him a block and a half away for those six years had been a great blessing. The last time I saw him laugh out loud was watching *National Lampoon's Vacation* that Christmas before he died. I'd never seen him get so tickled, laughing with his whole body. So those six years weren't all bad, but they weren't anything like we'd hoped for. Nonetheless, we had grown close. I'd forgiven my parents completely for the CCOC damage. What a special man. What an unfair ending.

Despite my questions and doubts, I grew closer to God during that period of grieving as I leaned on Him to renew my strength and help me carry on each day.

God Was Working; I Was Fretting

One Sunday at Garth Street Church, I introduced myself to a member of the worship team to encourage him for doing such a good job. As it turned out, he was a son of a South African missionary and was working to end human trafficking—a problem I didn't even realize existed. I was ashamed to learn that one in three porn websites shows images and videos of trafficked victims. Every time I had looked at porn to escape, I was guilty of enslaving young women. I had to make amends.

The missionary's son, Al, quickly became a family friend as I came to share the same passion for ending human slavery. His organization to combat human trafficking was just getting started but had a long-term goal of building a home where victims could recover and heal. Sherry and I got involved by sponsoring Al as a local missionary. The organization began to take shape with the development of articles of organization and bylaws. Sherry and I sat on the board of directors along with Al and his uncle. I thought perhaps this was how God would use our Old Albatross property.

Looking back at the enormous amount of time we spent, it's shocking how little we accomplished. The Old Albatross property proved to be too expensive to use for building a safe house. We visited other organizations, met with leaders of other safe houses, listened to police officers and social workers, and prayed and prayed. The idea of helping victims recover and heal seemed like a bright light of hope while I was grieving my father's death, managing a worsening marital conflict, and coping with what was becoming a deep disappointment in my career.

Our organization was convinced that we could build a haven of recovery from the PTSD, addiction, and spiritual desolation that plagued the victims of modern human slavery. I eventually found a suitable property. This seven-bedroom home had a perfect layout for establishing a safe home, and it came with fifty acres. Someone must have been building it for a large family when a financial disaster struck. Sherry and I purchased it with plans to donate it when the organization was ready to start working directly with victims. We figured it would take a few years to be ready, and I wanted the mortgage paid by then. Our home and lake home were already paid off, leaving the Old Albatross land and safe home as our only sources of debt.

The cart was definitely in front of the horse. Sherry was way too busy with work, but she still found a way to make it to most of the meetings. I was overextended with my surgical practice and couldn't devote the time needed to mentor Al. And somehow, we found time to paint the walls inside the safe home and purchase bedding for each bedroom. After a failed comedy night fundraiser, we gradually realized that Al was more of a visionary dreamer than a high-functioning nonprofit manager. We were committed to the idea of creating a safe home and considered finding a more capable person to carry out the vision. However, financial challenges arose at tax time, crushing any hope of continuing.

Under President Obama's leadership, the Centers for Medicare and Medicaid Services reduced the reimbursement of total hip and knees by 10 percent, and the IRS increased my taxes by 15 percent. I trusted my accountant to keep me prepared for April 15, so I had aggressively paid down $150,000 of principal on our safe home. My heart was bent toward giving. I enjoyed helping the poor and less fortunate. I wanted to see more and more people come to know and love Jesus. Maybe some part of my giving was also my striving to make God happy with me, but for the most part, being charitable was just a part of who God had made me to be. He had gifted me with the ability to give generously and happily. However, I most definitely did not enjoy giving to our wasteful US government, which shocked me with a $100,000 tax bill right at a time when I'd made my family cash poor.

I had no idea how to raise enough money to cover a six-figure tax payment. Should I sell the lake house we never used anymore, take a loan against my life insurance investment, or sell the safe house? The lake house seemed expendable, but the safe house held the immediate capital needed. The government obviously wasn't going to wait for a house to sell, so we got a loan against our whole life insurance policies and put the lake house and safe house on the market.

As in all adversity, God had a plan. The safe house sold to the first person who showed interest. An organization called Teen Challenge bought it to start a drug-and-alcohol rehabilitation facility for young women with small children. There were only a few other facilities like it across the country. Teen Challenge became well-known in the 1960s for helping troubled young men rehabilitate while developing a relationship with Jesus Christ. The US government had investigated its success and reported that it was due to what they called "the Jesus effect."[1]

Teen Challenge had a global impact, and a local chapter dreamed of doing more. After several meetings, we worked out an affordable deal for them to purchase ten acres and the house. Our partnership with them included donating $50,000 to Teen Challenge to help them with the purchase price and holding a $130,000 note on the remaining forty acres free of payments until 2019. It was a win-win. We had our tax payment, and they had a place to start a new ministry.

Teen Challenge was up and running within three months, helping its first addicted mother. We were so happy to be a part of it. They were able to do in three months what we had been working three years to accomplish. It was confirmation that we needed to leave Al's organization. Our plans to do something big by ourselves from the ground up seemed silly now after witnessing Teen Challenge's swift success.

Another revelation from our failed effort was the great work being done at a local foster care ministry, Coyote Hill. I had

---

1 "A Summary of Teen Challenge Studies," Teen Challenge International, USA, PDF, Mercy House Adult & Teen Challenge, accessed October 15, 2025, https://mercyhouseatc.com/wp-content/uploads/2019/01/a_summary_of_teen_chal-lenge_studies.pdf.

met with them to learn about the ins and outs of managing a residential care facility. I was stunned by how generous they were with their time, but also how effectively they had created a safe place for abused or neglected children. The meetings with Coyote Hill convinced me that they deserved my support. Later, I was placed on their board of directors.

Drinking Under Duress

The beauty of seeing God work all of our charitable efforts for His glory was not enough to bring me peace. The war in my mind remained a killing field. I had switched from Lexapro to Paxil in my attempt to find relief. It helped some, but when people with mental illness start feeling better, at some point, they decide they don't need meds, and I was no different. The withdrawal symptoms were excruciating. I had the surreal feeling that I was wide awake while sleepwalking with chest pain and tingling in my hands and head.

My anxiety was through the roof. At one point, my behavior was so bad that everybody left our house and fled to my mom's for advice. Sherry called Dr. Shauder's office the next day to plead for help. After one month off Paxil, I restarted it, and the family drama disappeared. Meds brought external peace, but inside, my mind was a revving engine before the lights go out at the start of a Grand Prix.

So I did what I had always done when life was overwhelming. I went on a family beach vacation. For the most part, we had a great time, until I went to pay for a meal with a credit card at a restaurant that only took cash. Anxiously, we scrounged together enough to cover the meal and then visited Castillo de San Marcos. As I was driving back to the VRBO, I began experiencing tingling in my arms, chest, and feet. I kept quiet about it, hoping it would fade, but then I began having facial spasms where the corners of my mouth were retracting against pursed lips. I could hide it no longer. I pulled over and told Sherry to drive me to a convenience store for Gatorade, thinking I possibly had low blood sugar. The drink did nothing for me. I had difficulty talking and difficulty swallowing.

Sherry quickly drove to an urgent care doctor while I started to have excessive tears and right eyelid fasciculations. Our kids were terrified and asked if I was having a stroke. I had no answer. As I walked, assisted from the car to the doctor's front door, I wondered if they might be right. My chest was tight, and my breathing was shallow. The doctor thought I could be having an allergic reaction to mold or a bug bite on my left thigh. He ran labs, which all came back normal.

After asking about my life and stressors, he decided to give me ten milligrams of IV Valium. When I awakened an hour or two later, I felt better—until he told me I may have had a conversion reaction (a condition where a mental health issue causes real, uncontrollable physical symptoms). He was so gentle and kind about it. He recommended that I find ways to alleviate stress, such as yoga, which had worked well for him. So I was officially and certifiably unhinged—great!

I remember thinking, *What if it happens again? What if it happens while operating? I'm screwed!* One thing was clear. I was facing the real possibility of being disabled and incapable of performing surgery ever again. That thought enraged me. I loved operating and helping people walk.

I began praying, "Please, Father, whatever it was, heal me, restore me, make me sane, let me continue to operate, remove all the worry and concern over this event. Father, help me trust you in all things, and then I'll have peace."

When I returned home, I only told my nurse practitioner about the incident. I promised her that if I began to feel anything similar while operating, I would let her know early enough for her to have one of my partners cover the case. Thankfully, that never happened, perhaps because I took the doctor's advice and started yoga. But the stressors continued.

Practicing medicine had been reduced to a sea of acronyms: MU-1/2/3 (Meaningful Use stages for electronic health records), PQRI (Physician Quality Reporting Initiative), CPOE (Computerized Physician Order Entry), ICD-10 (tenth revision of the International Classification of Diseases), P4P (pay-for-performance), HIPAA (Health Insurance Portability and Accountability Act), RAC (Recovery Audit Contractor), BPCI (Bundled Payments for Care Improvement), and CJR (Comprehensive Care for Joint Replacement). I could go on.

It seemed like practicing medicine was all about saving money through more regulation. Gain sharing. Bundled Payments. Comanagement of orthopaedic service line. Insurance peer-to-peer reviews. Unending new programs defined modern American healthcare. I still managed to help people, but it was destroying my body and spirit. Yoga was an incomplete fix. Foolishly, I turned to a more regular intake of whiskey.

Since I'd had my first drink at fourteen, my taste for alcohol had steadily increased. Drinking gave me a recurring existential crisis, which involved shaming myself, vowing abstinence, and eventually returning to the joy of beer, wine, and spirits. Occasional drunkenness had not yet become habitual. I just enjoyed a few on occasion (and at times, daily). It didn't matter how much or how little I drank; every drop tortured my conscience.

My "Puritan" CCOC mindset convinced me that I was on a slippery slope. Out of fear of alcoholism, I would periodically fast from booze. That meant ridding the house of it completely, throwing away my bar stock, and wasting money. Then, of course, I would eventually get stressed, buy more alcohol, and start drinking again.

Columbia Orthopaedic Group was spending millions of dollars to keep up with the government's unending spew of regulations. We spent millions on the first electronic health record only to find it incompatible and noncompliant a few years later. So we spent millions more on the second electronic medical record software. To save money, we gave up the ease of medical dictation for the less expensive but more inefficient voice recognition software. It was awful to use, but we had to use it in order to comply with governmental demands that we make notes available immediately. Our entire way of doing business was in flux.

The rapidly changing pace of my industry, combined with the constant fighting with my wife and kids, was soul-crushing. Despite reading hundreds of Christian books, daily Bible reading, praying, and journaling, I couldn't sense any spiritual changes that would ease my suffering. But whenever I relaxed with an ice-cold beer in my hand, I found I could escape to that carefree fifteen-year-old version of me who didn't give a damn about anything. I eventually resolved to be at peace with the sinlessness of moderation, but I doubted that my peace would ever feel complete.

Financial and family peace also seemed elusive. In the bad tax year, we sold everything we could to increase cash flow and reduce financial responsibilities. The recreational lake home had become useless to us, so the sell-off included the lake house. We invested with a couple of opportunists on spec homes, and we wound up selling a few houses before deciding not to build anymore due to the market circumstances. So, we sold the remaining lots and realized a 10 percent gain on our desperate gamble. Not bad, but not as great as we'd hoped.

Letting go of the lake house was the most painful sacrifice for our family. All of our good memories with family and friends were left behind in one day. I now spent my time running the kids around and watching them play sports. Times were definitely changing, and not for the better.

Wounded Healer

There's a country song by Little Big Town called "Your Side of the Bed" that came to define my marriage. Sherry did not appreciate my comparing this song to our marriage. Her defensiveness prevented her from fully grasping the magnitude of the problem. Even my mom, who calls herself an ostrich because she tends to stick her head in the sand, confessed that she feared we were headed for divorce. Sherry and I were failing.

Ironically, I decided to teach a marriage class at Garth Street Church when my own marriage was at its worst. Learning was always my go-to remedy when I felt anxious and stressed, and this instance was no different. My desire for control led me to read voraciously, thinking that more information would give me more control to solve my marriage woes. I chose to teach John Gottman's *Seven Principles for Making Marriage Work*. I wanted to explore the commonalities between Gottman's research-based book and biblical teaching. Though it was a helpful class with excellent insights, Sherry and I remained stuck.

We were living parallel lives. Affection was infrequent. Depression left me with little interest in sex, but when we did reunite, it was, as it always had been, spectacular. That helped, but it obviously wasn't enough.

Then a mentor introduced me to Jerry Bridges's book *Trusting God*. As I read it, my heart changed as I saw more clearly that God was good, that He loved me, and that He could be trusted. Although my relationship with Sherry was distant, I was closer to truly knowing God.

During this trying time, Garth Street Church decided to ordain me as an elder. This, too, seemed ironic, but I was excited nevertheless. CCOC boys are taught that man's ultimate purpose, the pinnacle of all spirituality, is to become an elder. Growing up, we were taught to live in a way that meets all the requirements for elders listed in Paul's letters to Timothy and Titus. Meeting all of those requirements is no easy feat, which is why I was rarely in a church with elders—no one qualified.

Garth Street had a different approach that made more sense. They taught that the biblical requirements represented the ideal man God wanted to lead His church, but they acknowledged that no one could ever live up to all of those qualifications perfectly. So they chose another imperfect servant in me. I debated and prayed and came to accept that this was God's next step for me.

Two expansions of church facilities and exhausting monthly meetings seemed worth the cost for the opportunity to offer some pastoral care to those who needed it. In the spirit of James 5, we prayed and anointed the sick with oil, including congregants fighting brain cancer, melanoma, marital strife, the loss of a son in the midst of his mother's own battle with cancer, and so on. Of course, it wasn't God's will to heal everyone we prayed over, but He did miraculously heal one man.

That man's name was Timothy, and he had metastatic melanoma in his lungs. Timothy was gentler than anyone I've ever known. He worked at a nonprofit, which was a natural fit for him, and he was good at it. He once encouraged me to stop being so private about my charitable giving because it robs people of the encouragement they need.

When he met with us, he was cachectic, a ghost of his former self. He hadn't been given much time to live. His kids were the same ages as my kids, and his family was desperate. We were desperate. It was my first elder prayer for healing, and I took it quite seriously that "a prayer offered in faith" could bring healing. He sat in a chair, as the elders surrounded him, anointed him with oil, and laid hands on him. We prayed for an hour. In the weeks that followed, he slowly improved until his cheeks were full of color and his body had gained weight. Ten years later, Timothy is still alive and doing well.

Healing Family Wounds

How could I trust God's power to answer prayer and bring healing for others while still needing Him to work in my own life and marriage? Sherry and I had reached a low point, and we didn't know how much longer we could go on. We started marriage counseling with a therapist named Elizabeth, the mother of one of Spencer's old basketball teammates. We liked and trusted her immediately. We spent the summer of 2015 focusing on fixing our marriage, and God showed up in a big way.

The therapist was the voice that God used to speak understanding into our situation. Gradually, the real dynamics of our marriage became clear to us. When I was pissed at Sherry's workaholism, I tended to shut her out. When Sherry saw me shutting her out, she made herself busier, thinking I just needed time to cool off. When she made herself busier, I got more pissed off. We were locked in this crazy cycle, but Elizabeth saw it as evidence that we were indeed pursuing each other. That was encouraging to hear.

When I was passionate and angry about a problem—for example, with the kids—but Sherry remained calm, I felt she wasn't taking it seriously. My volatility clashed with Sherry's patient attitude. I became angrier at her calm demeanor, while she just shut down. Elizabeth pointed out to Sherry that she only needed to acknowledge my feelings, not let them shut her down. She needed to express that she saw and understood my frustration. I needed to learn that Sherry did not need to show the same level of anger to sympathize with my frustration. Then we could decide together whether we were ready to discuss the issue, and each of us needed to feel free to table it if one of us wasn't ready.

Most importantly, at least to me, Elizabeth helped me realize that good marriages require a certain level of healthy dependency. I had so much concealed (and unconcealed) anger over the simple fact that when Sherry and I weren't right, nothing in life seemed right. To the counselor, it was normal, but to me, it didn't seem normal. I fought it. Sometimes, it bothered me so much that I would listen to Eddie Vedder and daydream about dying alone like the kid in the movie *Into the Wild*. I even daydreamed that if Sherry died of cancer, life would be easier for me in the long run, but I knew that was a lie from Satan.

These were dark thoughts indeed, and I desperately needed a solution. I was dependent on Sherry, but I hated having to rely on her. Elizabeth eventually convinced me that God's plan for marriage was oneness and that I needed to accept God's truth lest I lose my marriage. Our interdependence, derived from our shared history and experiences, was something no one could replace. It was a tender sign of a marriage that had worked quite well at one time.

On the other hand, Sherry learned to respect my business savvy while remaining independent in her decisions. Even if it took a year or two, as it often did (and still does), she eventually learned to accept and act on my business advice, whether it was maintaining accurate inventory, practicing appropriate accounting, saving for taxes, hiring well, getting good insurance, or paying people generously.

By God's grace, Elizabeth's wise counsel, and our own efforts, Sherry and I gradually got back on track and began enjoying each other again. We even found a way to communicate about her work without fighting. In the end, I lost five years of my relationship with Sherry. What a waste!

Becoming Reformed

The emotional turmoil of all of this left me feeling exhausted. My legs were like lead weights every time I climbed up stairs. I had no energy, even though my thyroid and testosterone levels were normal. Despite improvements in my home life, I felt like a zombie at times. Dr. Schauder finally asked me to wear a monitor at night to see if I had sleep apnea. It seemed ridiculous that a trim guy like me could have this "morbidly obese person's problem," but I was wrong. After several tests, I was diagnosed with severe sleep apnea, which placed me at high risk for having a stroke in the middle of the night. I started using a CPAP machine in my mid-forties and within days felt better than I had felt in years. It even cured my migraines. A CPAP was not the sexiest way to go to bed, but my wife and I managed.

Unfortunately, the obstructive sleep apnea diagnosis was soon followed by gall bladder disease. Everything I ate seemed to make me sick, but on closer analysis, I was mostly affected by fatty food. A nuclear medicine scan confirmed the diagnosis. I failed to find relief with medications, so I had a laparoscopic cholecystectomy. My family and clinic partners teased me that I was on an "every-two-years" surgery plan. I was unamused.

Still, like a disillusioned, unhooked fish floundering in the grass, my mind was spinning out of control. Earlier, I had tapered very slowly off Paxil, and I made it through an entire year without psych meds. But I had to do something. A low dose of Paxil helped with sleep, but I could not tolerate the sexual side effects this time. Starting back on Wellbutrin gave the familiar headaches and insomnia, but a happier disposition. Elavil at night was mildly helpful for getting some sleep, despite the horrible cotton mouth in the morning. But the racy thoughts raged on, and Wellbutrin wasn't cutting it. I needed Zoloft to control the barrage of ruminations. I was a mental mess.

I just couldn't slow down, not with all the responsibilities of saving for college, making those hefty mortgage payments on Old Albatross, and squirreling away extra cash for a highly uncertain tax bill. At year-end, I added extra OR days in December to meet the needs of everyone who had met their high deductibles. But expenses were up in December, so I didn't make any extra dollars from my overtime. It was deeply discouraging to realize that even if I worked harder, which physically hurt more, I reaped nothing but more rumination.

At the same time, a lot of my racing thoughts came from internal conflict over being an elder. It didn't seem to be a good fit for me, not at that time and place in my life. God clearly called me to be a surgeon. I love to diagnose, cut, and cure. I was not a fan of the long meetings. I also felt hypocritical about my drinking.

More importantly to me, my theology had changed. The apologetical arguments of Reformed theologians rang true in my heart. The books and podcasts of authors like R. C. Sproul, Tim Keller, and Jerry Bridges boldly explained what the Bible said rather than trying to "explain away" the more difficult passages as the CCOC had done. There were some hard truths I found difficult to accept, but simply believing what the Bible said seemed more reasonable than trying to build elaborate arguments for getting around it. I was learning to accept the straightforward teachings of passages like Romans 8 and 9, and I found comfort in the simple truth that I am saved by grace alone through faith alone in Christ alone to the glory of God alone because that is what the Scripture alone says.

Chapter 22

At Last, a Calvinist—Sort of

Let Me Come Home

As I have known You
I see You but
I want to see You
For who You are
I want to believe
That You are love.

I want to be known
As You know me
I need to feel loved
As You love me
I want to be Yours
Safe in Your arms.

Make me feel good enough
To be loved

Good enough
To be Your son
Good enough
To let go
Of my fear
Of my shame.

Father cover me
In Your grace
In Your love
Make me
Good enough.

Let me come home
To You
Run to me
With open arms
Hold me close
Never let me go.

THE ONSET OF winter blues in late 2016 led me to a psychologist named Dr. Mark Smith. I hoped to find a different and perhaps broader perspective on my issues, and I thought he might dive deeper into the darkness of my mind, places Christian counselors had left untouched, unanalyzed. However, our first conversation was soul-crushing.

My belief that I grew up in a *Leave It to Beaver* Christian home had long since given way to an understanding that I'd actually grown up in a strict legalistic sect. Dr. Smith added a great deal to my understanding that day. In fact, according to him, I grew up without ever fully experiencing unconditional love, which is a prerequisite for forming secure attachments in life. After all, the CCOC demanded 100 percent conformity, lest I be damned.

That made sense to me, but then he also challenged my view of my parents. Dr. Smith opened my eyes to the fact that they had demanded conformity as well, lest I be rejected. In an effort to merit their love, I sought approval and perfection. According to Smith, my motive in life was to gain the love I'd lacked in childhood. Whether from God, family, friends, or society in general, I longed to please people to become lovable to them. Instead, he said I should do what was loving simply because I already was loved unconditionally by God, who is love. Finally, I got it. Don't behave fearfully to be loved; behave lovingly because you *are* loved.

When I considered all that I'd done in life out of fear rather than love, the first thing that came to mind was becoming an elder. I hadn't felt called to become an elder. I'd done it to earn others' approval. So what was the most loving thing I could do about it now? Well, if I were sure of God's unconditional love for me, then it seemed the best way to love myself was to resign. My burned-out life needed less responsibility, not more.

At the time, my soul needed shepherding more than I needed to shepherd others. And so, after much prayer and deliberation and with a carefully crafted letter to protect my integrity, I resigned from eldership on December 9, 2016. The greatest challenge lay ahead, changing all the wrong-headed religious beliefs I had imprinted on my family, beliefs like the following: "If you think differently, you are wrong. If you don't have religion all figured out, you are not OK. If you leave the Restoration Movement, you are condemned." The truth was that I didn't have it all figured out and didn't need to. I only needed to have faith and to trust in God.

I knew there would be a big fallout from my resignation, but with His grace and love, I trusted I would be OK. Better than

OK, if I left, I knew I'd be *free*! And doesn't that sound familiar? But this time it was different. I had a deeply felt conviction that I'd never feel fully confident in my eternal security until I dared to leave the brand of churches that my father and I had grown up in.

Jesus came to set us captives free, and it began on Christmas Day. That year's Christmas fell on a Sunday. I went to church that day, hopeful that God would meet me there with encouragement, but when I got there, I felt anxious. Actually, I was pissed off.

How could worshipping Jesus and His incarnation cause me anxiety? Because I knew my mom was at the CCOC that same day, likely hearing a sermon on why we shouldn't celebrate Christmas (as it turned out, that was not the sermon topic that Sunday). Not having her with us at Christmas worship felt like both an accusation from her and a self-condemnation on my part. Sunday holidays were reminders of our religious division. Every Mother's Day, Father's Day, and Easter were all reminders of the imprinted belief "if you are not with me, you are not OK."

In truth, that reminder surfaced every Sunday for me—sometimes consciously, sometimes just beneath the surface. My response was to pray often that my mother would know and experience God's grace. Gradually, she did. During one of my weekly visits, she told me she had made peace with my absence from the CCOC. She could see I was still a devout follower of Jesus, and that led her to trust God and rest in the assurance of my salvation. Even better, years later, she wrote in a birthday card that she had loved me unconditionally all my life and regretted not saying it as I was growing up. When I told her how much that card meant to me, she said, "David, there is not one thing you could ever do that would make me love you less." My prayer had been answered.

When we arrived at Grandma's house, my brother Dan was already there. As I approached the front door, I felt even more anxious and depressed. I had so much newfound hope thanks to my changing theological beliefs, but I couldn't stop focusing on the past. When I chased this feeling down the rabbit hole of rumination, I realized I still harbored unforgiveness toward the CCOCs. By the time I realized it, I was already ringing the doorbell.

Dan opened the door with his typical big smile and hug, his gentle voice speaking words of love and affirmation.

"It's good to see ya!"

We had a great day together. On that Christmas, I resolved to lay down my burden of having been spiritually abused by the CCOC and my parents. I decided to become a victor, no longer a victim.

From the outside looking in, that resolution may seem ridiculous. How could a wealthy surgeon with a practice full of patients who loved him (and vice versa) be a victim? How could somebody with good standing in the community, with a beautiful wife and family, and with no apparent serious illnesses, be a victim? My shame was crushing me. Shame about feeling sorry for myself. Shame about feeling like a victim, as if I'd been kidnapped and tortured. It's not like my church and my parents forced me to mainline heroin. So how could I act like the CCOC made me a victim? Shame on me.

I ruminated about this throughout the holidays. Winter always seemed to do this to me. The same old questions tormented me: *Why did my parents take me to that church? Why did it affect me so differently from Dan? What was wrong with me? How can those CCOC folks not see that they are exactly like the Pharisees? Maybe none of this matters. What if I just accept my weakness and learn to find power in Christ, like the apostle Paul did with his thorn in the flesh? Will I ever be free to live in peace? Will I ever give up the illusion that I need to be in control?*

One Sunday, while attending my brother-in-law's Assembly of God church, I paused my rumination to go forward and ask an elderly couple to pray for my healing. Despite my confusion over the "tongue speaking," I did understand a Martin Luther quote from one of them: "You cannot keep birds from flying over your head, but you can keep them from building a nest." Then I was encouraged to proclaim, "Spirit of anxiety and fear, I release you in Jesus's name!" I awkwardly complied. After that, the couple had me pronounce, "I am a free man! I am a free man! I am a free man!" Speaking English as well as a presumably angelic language, they laid hands on me and prayed again.

Finally, I walked back to my seat, feeling thankful, mildly disturbed, and mostly hopeful.

Despite this, I remained in fear and trembling over the next week as I pondered whether to leave the Restoration Movement churches for the Reformation Movement's churches. My immediate family was definitely on board with leaving. Sherry was supportive of whatever helped me most, though I'm sure there were limits. I had been watching the Crossing, a local evangelical Presbyterian church, worship service online for the past couple of months, and I was ready to investigate further. From what I'd seen, I'd concluded that one of the pastors, Miles, seemed like someone I could relate to. He liked politics, was well-read, and was passionate about Jesus.

I set up a meeting with Miles on a clinic day lunch break. We met at Houlihan's. I remember he ordered a salad, and I had salmon. My plan to keep the conversation light quickly faded. His aura of calm, gentle pastoral love disarmed me. Like a surgeon, he opened me up and wasted no time in exposing the truth. Every time I fought back tears, Miles would avert his gaze and take another bite of salad. Then he pressed on and helped me confront the harsh reality of what I'd been through.

Despite my efforts to be a victor, I was still a victim. I had suffered thirty-five years of spiritual abuse, which Miles said is no less victimizing than physical abuse. Worse yet, he said I would likely never fully get over it. However, instead of remaining a victim, he encouraged me to face the past, come to terms with it, and change my life. There was nothing I wanted more in life than to move on. I hated thinking of myself as a victim, but it kept coming up.

Miles never made it seem like he was pushing for me to go to his church. In a laidback manner, he encouraged me to think more about what was missing and what needed to change. The discussion of doctrinal issues was much shorter than that on relationships. Miles asked if I thought my lack of friends was a problem. It certainly was. I felt lonely.

Finally, Miles affirmed me by saying, "David, God is pleased with you. If He walked into this room right now, He would smile and be glad to see you."

Once I had regained my composure from such a graceful thought, I sought one more pearl of wisdom: "How do I leave Garth Street on good terms? I love those people." His answer was so good that I acted on it immediately. Within fifteen minutes, I was in the Garth Street lobby talking to Karl, who just happened to be studying in a lobby. A divine appointment.

I explained to Karl that I didn't think I could heal from my past unless I dared to leave the Restoration Movement entirely. If I was ever going to stop the endless rumination and anxiety, I had to follow my own spiritual path in search of peace with God and with my past. Karl first said he wanted to throw up a little. Then he said that, although he didn't want to guilt me, he thought Garth Street was stronger in kingdom work with me than without me.

After expressing our mutual love and hugging goodbye, I drove to my mom's house. Now was the time to break the news to her.

With a stern look, my mom's response to my announcement was, "Well, I'll never change!" I wasn't surprised. Eventually, she softened and told me she had been praying for peace about Dan and me and with our decisions about where to worship. She explained that she thought Dan and I were smarter than she was and vowed to respect our choices. Mom assured me that God had given her peace about it.

With that blessing, I left for home to journal about the day (until my carpal tunnel syndrome forced me to quit writing). A few months later, after resigning from the Independent Christian Church's youth organization board, I was completely free of my Restoration Movement roots.

Chapter 23

FINALLY FREE?

A Daughter for All Seasons

Alive in autumn
Beloved and new
Chosen to exist
By God and us, too

Born in the summer
A blessing, a girl,
Daddy's little girl!
Our own priceless pearl

Snuggles and kisses
Noon teas, bike riding
Trail hiking and house
Fishing, four-wheeling

Evening dinner talks
Tutoring, fighting
Counseling, coping
Striving, succeeding

Singing downstairs or
Alone in your room
You're pulling away
Becoming your own

So young and unsure
Am I good enough?
What do the boys think?
Why is this so tough?

True, God is enough
Yes, He set me free
But I want a man
Who loves me for me

Paige, do you see us?
Adoring parents
Who love you for you
We're not here by chance

Our love's unfailing
Our pride's limitless
You're more than enough
Do you believe us?

Well, here's what we think
From our watchful care

By observation
We humbly declare

Sensitivity
For the young and old
So compassionate
A beautiful soul

Funny and playful
Loyal and fierce
Pretty, so pretty
A vision of bliss

Your strong work ethic
Propels you forward
Your perseverance
Sustains your reward

Patient to find friends
Who are kind like you
Graceful, forgiving
Loving, selfless, too

Believer in Christ
Faithful to our God
A friend to Jesus
A neighbor to all

A soft gift to us
Pure love from the start
Daily in our pray'rs
Always in our heart

One day to depart
With God's chosen man
The one we've prayed for
Asked us for your hand

Remember our time
The good and the bad
Shaped you, molded you
See the plan God had?

You'll be a great wife
A sweet mother, too
Strong, independent
Gentle, humble, true

Alive in autumn
Born in the summer
Blossoming in spring
Blessing our winter.

A T A GREATLY appreciated follow-up appointment, Miles invited me to reread Keller's *Prodigal God*. After a month, we met in his office once or twice to discuss it. The main lesson for me was that I tended to be the self-righteous older brother in Jesus's parable of the prodigal son. The father invited the angry older brother to his younger brother's homecoming party. The Bible does not reveal his answer, but the point is clear. The self-righteous Christians are in far more peril with God than the repentant, sinful ones.

Miles said I needed to repent of any good works that were done to earn God's favor and live in a position of grace before God. It sounded a lot like what my psychologist had said. Repenting of good works was not a familiar concept to me, but I understood it meant a change in my attitude about why I do good. In other words, do I obey to twist God's arm into finally approving of me, or do I do it out of an abundance of joy, knowing that God's grace approves me?

Soon after we started attending the new church, we began their Discovery Class to learn more about what they believed, or more importantly, about *who* they believed the Bible teaches that God is. By now, I was used to reading and contemplating Reformed theology, so I was entranced. However, Sherry was less intrigued. She had strong beliefs about who God is supposed to be, and for her, they were heartwarming and pleasant. I, on the other hand, was eager to learn about a God who was good, who loved me, yet who maintained total control of all the chaos of life. I was exhausted with my efforts to control it. It was freeing to believe that the Bible meant what it said about God's sovereignty and humbling to realize that every aspect of my life did not depend completely upon me.

This mindset did not carry over into my parenting, not right away. I was still a control freak. I learned later that shame motivates no one. I should have known better by now.

Jay, another pastor at the Crossing, helped me tremendously when we met to discuss how to be a better parent. He said I should never confuse someone's present moral behavior with their ultimate salvation. That insight tipped my scale. My beliefs were in such a state of flux that I didn't know what to think except that I equated morality with salvation. Maybe that's why I never felt saved. I knew I was not morally perfect. Jay had to explain the gospel to me all over again.

As he explained, Jesus did what we could not do: live a morally perfect life. He who had no sin took on our sins and then gave up His life as an atoning sacrifice. When we have faith in His atoning work, we take on His righteous, perfect moral record. This substitu-tionary atonement meant that I was a passive recipient, something that seemed un-American to me. I still wanted to earn it and feel like I deserved it. Thank God His offer of grace is un-American! God's grace and love brought health where judgment, condem-nation, and shame had caused spiritual sickness. And with that, my parenting style took a dramatic turn toward grace.

Searching for Peace Amid Burnout

Could it be that God was doing the same in my life? I was too depressed from dealing with my adult children to feel it at the time. At the same time, my work life had only gotten worse as I had to deal with more regulations and more time interfacing with inefficient technology. Dictating into voice "un"-recognition software while poorly editing a clinic note often had me cursing and punching the wall.

Because my dictation booth was next to a clinic room, I had a younger partner come next door and ask if I was OK. I lied and told him I was fine. Despite seeing God more clearly, I was still mentally suffering more and more. I begged God to bring healing, but I got none. My anxiety and depression worsened. Why didn't more spiritual understanding bring more mental health? I mistakenly still thought they were related.

I had moments of clarity and freedom in Christ, times when I felt His acceptance despite my flaws, felt His faithfulness despite my doubts. Galatians 1:10–24 spoke straight to my heart that I was set apart before birth and called by God, who was pleased to reveal His Son to me. The reformed sermons consistently urged me to place myself in God's story and live a bigger life. I was trying to. I wanted nothing more than to be convinced that God had made me grow up in a spiritually abusive home to draw me passionately to Himself.

Yet my damnable, disordered thinking was proving nearly impossible to reorder. I was meeting monthly with a psychologist, seeking wisdom to sort through my past, present, and future. The simplicity of "do what is loving because God is love" and "do your best and know that it was enough" gave me much-needed clarity about my journey toward God, eased my suffering, and helped me accept His love.

However, we talked in circles about how to deal with my burnout. The bottom line was that I had chronic depression with anxiety, and even with the best cognitive behavioral tools, I realized I might always have a battle before me. Nonetheless, I gathered insight from the psychologist with the same fervor as kids chasing after candy at a parade.

One day, he had me list all (and he meant all) of my expectations in life. After a few pages of multiple columns on legal paper, I saw how clearly ridiculous my expectations were. I had always thought it was weak when my dad would tell me to lower my expectations. As it turns out, he was spot on. From the psychologist, I learned mindfulness, stress management, and how to embrace change with less fear. But it wasn't enough.

With all the psych medication changes, my doctor ordered labs and found my liver function tests were abnormally high. I couldn't believe it! Was I really drinking that much? I fasted from alcohol for two weeks and had another test, which showed that my LFTs had returned to normal. Clearly, my alcohol consumption was the problem. What was I doing to myself? What was this job doing to me? I only had myself to blame. Though I felt closer to Jesus and more accepting of God's sovereign love, I was living miserably from vacation to vacation and despising the work time in between.

"If you are that miserable, why don't you just quit?" Sherry would often ask.

Unfortunately, my income was too high to give up. Our lifestyle and charitable work were too important to give up. Surely God had gifted me so I could do what few can do, to earn what few can earn, and to share like few can share. God needed me to do this, right?

I thought maybe I would be happier in a better climate, at a better practice with a slower pace, but I couldn't find any of those things online. Searching for the sunniest US cities with less demanding orthopaedic jobs and no on-call responsibilities proved fruitless. Hours spent searching for a quiet farm with a stocked pond were wasted. I needed a new me, not a vacation, not a different house or more land. I needed a new me.

Falling Apart, Hoping for More

Throughout 2017, as I suffered from these thoughts, I was also suffering from a chronic cough. It got to the point where I couldn't lie flat without coughing so hard I choked. If I watched a comedy and laughed, I would have the same response. I had to quit yoga because anytime I was head-down, same response. The first half of the year was spent mistreating my cough caused by bronchitis while investigating alternative causes. Secretly, I hoped it was something terminal. What a great exit that would be from all my suffering and what a glorious entrance into the arms of God!

Ultimately, the culprit proved to be laryngeal pharyngeal reflux. Diet and lifestyle changes, along with medicine, did nothing. I just coughed all year long with no relief. What a miserable way to live.

In December, I had a repeat laparoscopic Nissen fundoplication to correct the problem. I'd had the procedure before, seventeen years earlier, and it had been a horrifying experience. I had wretched and wretched in extreme pain for days afterward. How could I go through that again?

Sherry and I, along with her brother and wife, went to Sandals Grand Bahamian in October, just before the surgery. I spent most of the time slightly intoxicated and meditating on Psalms 23, and to my surprise, I found God's peace in the midst of my impending suffering.

God is my loving shepherd, tending to my safety with watchful care. He meets all my needs, even the needs I don't recognize, like rest and tranquility. He restores me, leads me, and goes with me through every dark valley. He blesses me and abundantly provides for me right in front of my enemies. He gives me a certain future with Him filled with His goodness and mercy forever. How could I fear in the face of such a wonderful truth? And for a while, I didn't.

Praise God, the surgery went beautifully! I even went on a New Year's trip to Chicago that I had planned for the family. While they ate like kings and queens, I was limited to soup and baby food. Still, we had fun, and I felt particularly close to God—until the train ride home. It was chaos at Union Station, and I had another severe conversion reaction just like I'd had at the Castillo de San Marcos in Florida. Thinking it might be hypoglycemia, I ate three sugar packets. Then I chewed up a full Xanax and focused on my breathing for a few minutes. We finally found the train, and I made it home without seeking medical help.

It seemed like highs were always followed by lows. Such is life. Sadly, the mental gains just didn't last. Psalms 16, 29, 30, and 31 spoke so loudly to me. God is faithful. Eventually, I'll be OK, without pain, without doubt, without depression. One day, I will be in His presence, face-to-face, beholding His glory in a newly resurrected body, experiencing the fullness of joy with pleasures forevermore. I clung to that hope by reading voraciously and seeking rest in His promises.

The peace that reading brought was often eclipsed by pain of some sort. In 2018, I quit performing total hip arthroplasty, hoping to avoid the neck, shoulder, and back pain that such procedures caused me. It was a big step, a leap of faith that seemed to help a bit.

Continuing on the roller coaster of highs and lows, my hands began bothering me in 2018 as well. My mom, who had hated to see me suffer so many problems related to my job, finally asked me if I thought God was trying to tell me something, like the old joke about the flood victim stranded on his rooftop who keeps refusing help from people because he's waiting on God to rescue him miraculously.

If God was trying to tell me something, I clearly wasn't listening (or hearing Him).

Chapter 24

HOPE AND FUTURE?

Longing

"It's still so hard," he cries
As I reach for his hand and reply
"I cannot even imagine."
I can only be still and listen.

He tells of happy times
He shares their struggles
They have overcome together
They have loved each other.

Through blurry eyes I see
A nearly broken man before me
Broken but for the hope that remains
To one day see her and hold her again

Together in the presence of our Father
Face-to-face with our Savior
The Spirit within us whispers
Comfort for temporal lovers

"You are not alone or forsaken.
I will come again
To save you from your sorrow.
A heavenly reunion awaits some glad tomorrow."

WHETHER AS A teenager in high school or a young man in college, I had delivered many sermons in my little Conservative Churches of Christ. My preaching elicited the same response: "You missed your calling; you should have been a preacher." Even as a physician speaking at the two men's conferences that I coordinated, I received similar compliments. I never thought much of them until a Catholic Christian physical therapist said the same thing after hearing me pray with a patient.

As I began looking back, I could see that I had a gift outside of orthopaedics. I had taught Sunday school to all age levels throughout my adult life at big and small churches, and teaching felt as natural as cutting open a knee. Pastor Miles had seemed pretty confident that I could teach eternal security better than I could accept it personally. But that was then; now that I had graciously accepted my personal, unchangeable security, was God calling me to use this gift of teaching? Was that why He allowed so many physical problems—to cause me to pivot from operating to teaching?

Before the dark, snowy, depressing winter of 2018 began, Jay invited me to join the leadership track at church. For nine months, every Wednesday, we would meet and dive deeper into God's word while developing relationships with a small group of like-minded men. My old CCOC thinking and fear of expectations were still tripping me up, but I decided to dive in and loved it. There were no strings attached, just a loving church seeking to train up leaders.

I had already read a few books on the calling to ministry that year and listened to some podcasts on the topic. With my reduced surgical workload, I felt compelled to learn more about what it truly means to be called. One thing stood out in my study—your calling needs to be affirmed by the church. I read and heard this from several sources, and it made sense to me based on my understanding of the book of Acts.

Then it happened out of the blue. One day, Jay invited me to join a small cohort of men at the church to take seminary classes online. That felt like a very specific calling to me! My heart had been broken enough to search more deeply about God, and my body had been broken enough to slow my practice down to make time for study. It was His timing, and I was all in.

Yet, no amount of spirituality or awakening to a calling seemed to soothe the deep, underlying mental damage or illness or whatever the hell it was. I upped my antidepressant dose in an effort to cope better with the increased anxiety of working with hand, wrist, and elbow pain. Overall, I think my mood improved, but it also seemed more erratic. No highs, just varying levels of lows, which at times got pretty dark, as I pondered death and the hopelessness of continuing to live.

How in the world could I be so blessed but my mind be so cursed? An added mood stabilizer left me restless, so much so that I couldn't even sit and read for more than ten minutes, which was unusual for me. I tapered off the mood stabilizer.

Was I just taking psych meds so I could keep doing something I no longer enjoyed? A patient told me that she'd become depressed at work when she had started helping a child with autism during lunch hour, which had proved very challenging. She had always been so good with kids, a real natural, but this new challenge felt like defeat. Then she was prescribed Lexapro. Suddenly, a whole new world opened up to her, and she was able to help that little boy with autism, and she even enjoyed doing so.

I wondered if I was like her. Would some miracle drug enable me to enjoy my work again? Or would I only have peace if I retired early and pursued another passion? Does God use mental illness to call someone to ministry? That seemed strange to me, but then again, He is the God who once used a talking donkey to communicate His wishes to a prophet, and many of those prophets seemed pretty depressed at times.

Maybe I was just holding on to my career in orthopaedics for the money. I loved the financial freedom it gave me, being able to buy what I wanted, do what I wanted, and give generously. Was God using my anxious, depressed mind to pry my slightly numb hands away from the money and turn my thoughts upward to Him? Or maybe it was all unrelated. Maybe there was some other answer out there, one I simply hadn't yet discovered? The ruminations would not stop.

What did God want from me? That question tormented me. Though I was professionally very successful, I felt like a failure. But I knew I was a child of God, dearly loved and eternally secure. "I am chosen, not forsaken." I had hope and a future. And maybe, just maybe, I had another calling.

Chapter 25

A HOLY MOMENT

New Life

So many times down though the ages,
Men and women have come together with special embraces.
The fruit of their deep and abiding love
Was a child, a gift from God above.
But not all special embraces are blessed with God's consideration.
Thus some lovers are left with the sorrow of no fruition.
Such was the case with your mother and father,
Yet they never gave in to their despair.
They clung to the hope of your conception,
And with the help of their noble physicians, hope was fulfilled
by your inception.
But you were not alone inside your mother's belly.
There were three others and one before you, but God saw fit to
take them early.
So while we celebrated your enduring,
We quietly mourned their passing.

Oh, how many times we prayed that God would keep you safe
from harm,
And throughout many months of worry, we leaned on His ever-
lasting arm.
Finally, the rapturous day of your birth did come and tears
filled our eyes,
And we fell to our knees in praise to God and countless prayers
did rise.
"We thank Thee, our Father, for the gift of this beautiful infant.
May she serve and love You as we do and may Your merciful
hand guide her every step.
May You fill her parents with understanding and wisdom,
And may their home be filled with love, joy, hope, and faith.
Amen."

ULTIMATELY, I THINK what God wanted from me is to have more moments in life like the following one.

We were about to go on a trip to the Ozarks, but I stopped at the car wash to clean my dirty truck before we left. After going through the car wash, I started to vacuum when I noticed a young man nearby. He was dressed more for a men's fashion magazine than a Midwest carwash.

Though the lightweight button-up shirt, tapered high-water trousers, and athletic Oxford shoes were quite fashionable, I noticed him because he was sprinting from one end of the vacuum stations all the way to the attendant's window. It seemed like odd behavior, especially when it was eighty-six degrees outside, and the humidity was as thick as molasses.

In a hurry, I kept vacuuming, but a few minutes later, the sprinting male model showed up right behind me, asking if he could borrow my cell phone. In a state of barely controlled panic, he said, "My daughter is locked in the car with my keys and cell phone."

I immediately unlocked my phone, handed it to him, and silently prayed for him and his child.

He called family and handed the phone back to me. At this point, I had observed that his vehicle was black and not running, so there was no A/C for the baby. If I'd been in his shoes, I would've been filling those Oxfords with my own urine as I panicked. But I wasn't in his shoes, so I stayed calm and tried to make small talk until help arrived.

Amid all the small talk, I encouraged him to believe the truth of the situation. "It was just a mishap, a mistake. It happens to us because we are human," I said. "It does not make you a bad husband or a bad father."

To his credit, he stayed pretty calm. He was about my kids' age, married, and his baby daughter was three and a half months old. Thankfully, the baby was sitting rather contentedly in the small black SUV despite the sunny day. However, we both knew that at some point, we might need to break the glass.

I asked him if he had called "momma," but he shook his head no. I encouraged him to do so and handed him my phone again. While he stood talking on the driver's side of the SUV, I walked over to the passenger's side to check on the baby. She was super cute and smiled. I suddenly became self-conscious about being a fully bearded, bald man. What if the baby started crying because a scary-looking man was cooing at her?

Thankfully, she stayed happy. As the father handed the phone back to me, I asked him if he got "grief or grace" from the baby's mom. He would only admit that his wife was "concerned." All in all, I found him to be an impressive young man.

Still, no one had arrived to help, and the baby had fallen asleep. Finally, we decided to call 911. I was out of time. My family was supposed to be in Springfield at a specific time. I also didn't want this young father to wait alone.

At the same time, God was prompting me to do more for this young father. I weighed the risk of alienating the man I was trying to help against the risk of missing an opportunity to see God at work. In faith, I chose the latter. I boldly asked the father if he was a praying man, and he responded, "Yes, I am."

As soon as I said, "Well, let's pray," he placed his hand on my shoulder, and together we bowed our heads. I felt the need to pray specifically for his family, that this scary situation would bring them together in peace as they saw God's faithfulness, goodness, and love. We gave glory to God, as I acknowledged that He is sovereign, and He was involved in this very situation to bring glory to Himself and goodness to us who love Him. I asked God to use this as an opportunity to grow our faith and trust in Him.

Without being specific, I was asking God not to let the situation end in a marital spat. After the "amen," we lifted our heads and saw a guy approaching us from the adjacent vacuuming bay. He said he'd wanted to wait until we were "done talking" to offer help. As it turned out, he was a retired firefighter and always kept the equipment in his truck to help people who had locked their keys in their cars! The door was open within two minutes of our amen!

In the end, the father thanked me, shook my hand, looked me in the eye, and said, "Wow, this was a holy moment!"

Indeed it was! Maybe moments like this were all God wanted from me, simply to follow Micah 6:8: "He has told you, O man, what is good; and what does the Lord require of you but to do justice, and to love kindness, and to walk humbly with your God?"

Chapter 26

THE SHADOW OF DEATH

South Mountain

I feel like I'm going to do something big with my life
He said
I used to think that too
I replied
What? You don't think you have?
Not really.
You don't think helping thousands of people walk is really big.

Hmmm
Winter depression has been deep
Too deep to see the good being done at the surface
Atop South Mountain I pray
Waiting for a sense of presence and hoping for a word of
encouragement
I consider for what I'm to be grateful
Eventually, I notice my hands

I hold them out and ponder what they have done
Has it been really big?

These hands have operated on thousands of hips and knees
Delivered babies
Placed IVs in veterans
Taken Sherry's hand in marriage
Held my babies
Prayed over the sick and dying
Held my dying father's hand
Comforted my mother as she grieved
These hands have been raised in praise
Folded in prayer
Held by comforting pastors
Prayed over hundreds of patients hand in hand
Taken a patient's hand in prayer and had fear leave her instantly—
Her words, not mine

These hands are a really big deal, a gift from my loving Father God.
They have given much to ministry
Guided children in nurseries
Led children in youth groups
Openly received our Father's good and perfect gifts
I rejoice and I will continue to rejoice
I feel the sadness lifting
I think it's gone
At least at this moment, sitting atop South Mountain

L IFE GETS DREARY without adequate sleep. Clarity is lost. Hope fades. Reality becomes surreal. My sleepless hours due to hand numbness and paresthesias were compounded by my weakening grip strength. I had to do something, but as a surgeon, pondering having surgery on my own elbows and wrists was like having an out-of-body experience. It's too optimistic to say I felt like I was circling the drain. Actually, I felt like I was lost in a dark cave, groping for a way out.

Dr. Shauder tapered me off Zoloft and started me on Effexor, and at the same time, I committed to cutting back my surgical load from four cases a day to three. Gradually, my neck and back began to feel better. It was like sunlight breaking forth in that dark cave. Unfortunately, my hands continued to worsen, interfering with my sleep every night. My mood was better, but only temporarily.

After treating a left wrist triangular fibrocartilage complex tear and pisotriquetral arthritis with injections, my hand surgeon partner discerned that my cubital tunnel syndrome must be the primary cause of the left wrist pain. He eventually discovered that I had both bilateral carpal and cubital tunnel syndromes. I tried braces, pills, and carpal tunnel steroid injections that year, to little effect. Within months, despite the wonderfully brilliant sunshine of spring, my world grew dark again. I was back in the cave of misery with no apparent way out.

I began having frequent suicidal thoughts. I knew it was time to make some changes. Despite all of my efforts, my nerve problems kept getting worse. At this point, even standing with my arms crossed or lying down in the fetal position to sleep was no longer comfortable. It was so bad that I couldn't hold a book without my hands going to sleep, both from the ulnar and median nerve compression. My only remaining hobby was being taken away from me. Work was more of a nuisance than ever.

Finally, in June 2019, I had surgery. I had right-hand carpal tunnel release and cubital tunnel release with submuscular ulnar nerve transfer. This was followed two weeks later by the same surgery on the left hand and elbow.

Recovery was a long, hellacious month of elbow and wrist immobilization in painful splints. The right side recovered beautifully. The left side, however, experienced intermittent numbness in the ring and little fingers. This had been partly expected from my pre-operative EMG/NCS, which showed I already had mild chronic left ulnar neuropathy. The left wrist pain gradually returned, but was now mostly isolated to the arthritic pisotriquetral joint. My mind began spinning out of control, horrified at the thought that my surgery had failed and that I might need a re-operation to avoid living with numbness and painful paresthesias.

I began having darker thoughts.

Why live like this? I wondered. *In death, I will see my Creator and Savior face-to-face. Living just means pain. Death would bring relief.*

But how would I do it? A combat shotgun shoved up under my left rib cage should bring a quick end to my cardiovascular system. The hanging scene from the Lady Gaga/Bradley Cooper remake of *A Star is Born* seemed like a cleaner way to go. Listening to the *Into the Wild* soundtrack made poison berries seem like a good option. Then again, as a man, my suicide should be violent, shouldn't it? Only women use pills and overdose. Still, it sounded so much more peaceful, unless it didn't work.

These thoughts tormented me constantly, but ultimately, I couldn't do it. I love my family too much. I couldn't put them through the pain. I was ashamed for even pondering such nonsense. Nevertheless, I returned to such thoughts again and again. I knew I had to tell someone.

Instead, I started drinking more. More often than not, I washed down pain pills with whiskey or beer. Taking tramadol helped with the nerve pain during recovery, but that small bit of relief wasn't enough to stop me from downing four or five drinks nightly in search of more relief. I knew better than to combine tramadol and bourbon, as both can make seizures more likely, but the confident doctor that I was, I thought, "Oh, I can handle it." I just kept drinking and waited to recover, and thankfully, avoided having a seizure.

My physician, Dr. Shauder, decided it was time for me to see a psychiatrist. That decision enraged me. I felt disgusted that someone as bright and successful as I was needed to seek professional help for suicidal thoughts. I felt ashamed, weak, helpless, and foolish. Yet, the fact remained, I needed a psychiatrist. I needed help, so I went. I couldn't imagine what a ninety-minute meeting could reveal that would improve my situation. I had already tried several different antidepressants, mood stabilizers, and anxiolytics. Some had worked but only for a short time. Others made my life worse, and the withdrawal side effects were hell. Alcohol seemed like the best medicine, but it only offered temporary relief, along with unhealthy consequences.

I decided to give psychiatric medications another try, so I met with Dr. Peri, my psychiatrist, in August, the same month that I started my seminary cohort. She listened to my story. I told her everything, including my self-diagnosed moderate alcohol use disorder while on pain pills during my surgery recovery. While she was relieved that I only used the pills during recovery and not while working, she was clearly unhappy with my alcohol intake. Still, she didn't judge or shame me for it.

After looking over my Genomind test results, which showed how my genetic makeup affects my response to different classes of medications, she decided to taper me off Effexor and put me on Viibryd. She also explained that I needed Deplin, an L-methyl folate supplement. Before setting a follow-up appointment a month later, she asked a simple question:

"What's it going to take for you to give yourself a break?"

Reading Larry Crabb's *Inside Out* simultaneously with A. W. Tozer's *Pursuit of God* had me asking myself the same question. Together, these two books opened my mind to the idea that joy lies in accepting the stark reality of life's inherent imperfections while remaining aware of God's abiding presence. Wealth, family, success, and reputation are not guarantors of happiness and contentment. Everything in this world is flawed, and to the hypercritical, those flaws may preclude joy. But God provides the path to joy. I learned to accept that a fallen world functions with flaws and to know that I AM is with me and will make all things new eventually and eternally. Perhaps, armed with these insights, I could finally give myself a break and find peace of mind.

At the same time, the idea that I might have a calling outside of medicine seemed more likely to be the break I needed. It would mean freedom from the emotional and physical demands of surgery, along with its toll on my mind and body. My first seminary class was Covenant Theology, and it awakened in me a greater trust in God's faithfulness to His promises. The men in the group seemed like good people, and I looked forward to getting to know them better. Our discussions encouraged me even more about what the future might hold.

Or maybe it was just the Viibryd and Deplin working. Either way, winter was coming.

A Little Help from My Friends

My self-inflicted pressure to excel slowly turned my seminary class from joy to stress. I began holing up in my office, reading and studying during every spare moment. The weather was starting to change from Missouri's typical two to three weeks of pleasant fall weather to a rainy, cold prewinter. It matched my changing mood.

Dr. Peri congratulated me on successfully weaning off Effexor (though Sherry probably would have disagreed that it was successful, given my ridiculous volatility during the change). The doctor then increased my Viibryd to the maximum dose, which only added to my irritability. Sherry begged for a change, and my mind begged for relief from the constant fluctuation in chemicals. Once again, suicide began to seem like a reasonable solution. Strangely, suicide seemed hopeful. As my thoughts turned dark, only nightly bourbon brought relief.

I had a hermeneutical paper due and a group oral final exam looming. Still, my new sense of calling to a master of arts in biblical and theological studies (MABTS) soon began to fade. In my surgical practice, my new probationary associate, Derek, suddenly seemed on the verge of losing his career before it even began.

My practice had hired Derek as a new joint replacement surgeon, and he took on some of my workload. Finally, my life seemed well balanced between my competing interests in seminary and surgery. Derek got off to a great start, but three months in, he had a stroke. He was only thirty-two years old. It was shocking, and somehow it dislodged the morbid suicidal thoughts from my mind.

I had to step up. For surgeons, winter is the busiest time of the year. Many patients have met their out-of-pocket deductibles, so they start scheduling their expensive surgeries before the year ends.

Unfortunately, health insurance premiums and deductibles were skyrocketing to all-time highs. A knee replacement was guaranteed to hit your maximum out-of-pocket expenses. So it was more important than ever for patients to get procedures done by the end of the year. For most people in mid-Missouri, paying the maximum out-of-pocket two years in a row would be financially crippling. As a partnership, we decided not to let that happen to Derek's patients. There were four of us remaining joint surgeons, so we divided up Derek's surgical case load for November and December to ensure patients would have surgery before the year ended.

(Side note: It would be great if deductibles reset on your birthday, eliminating this end-of-the-year rush.)

I soon found myself immersed in more knee replacements than I could physically handle, leaving me with no margin to take my online seminary class for credit. I was forced to switch tracks to "audit only." Trudging through the long weeks of surgery, I continued the class under no pressure to perform. In a way, it was a big relief, but it cast doubt upon my new calling, as this was the second time I had failed to complete a seminary class for credit.

As winter droned on with cold darkness, my disappointment was matched only by my despair. Every afternoon and evening, I'd surround my neck and back with ice, causing my wife to question why I kept operating if it made me suffer as if I were an NFL lineman. I began to have grave fears about what would happen if I reached a point where I could no longer perform surgery. What was my out? When could I retire? What would I do in early retirement? Would auditing an MABTS degree merit any consideration for future ministerial work? Would my mind ever slow down long enough to be happy? Was I still drinking too much?

In December, still having suicidal ideations and looking for answers, I met with pastor Miles. He pointed out that life was meant to be lived in community.

"Who are your close friends?" he asked.

I struggled to name two people.

"You can't just hole up in your house and expect to find fulfillment in the pages you read," he said.

I'd gotten to a point where I really didn't spend any time with any close friends outside of work. All I did was walk my dogs and read. He counseled me about friendship and how to foster those relationships. Honestly, it was embarrassing, made me feel terribly alone, and pissed me off that the only help he had to offer at my lowest point was to make friends. It seemed overly simplistic and dismissive, but deep down, I knew he had offered wisdom.

At my psychiatry follow-up, Dr. Peri put me back on Zoloft while tapering me off Viibryd. She described Zoloft as "the little black dress of psychiatry" because it's always appropriate. She thought the Deplin would improve my response to Zoloft this time. Thankfully, she was right, and slowly my thoughts migrated away from dark contemplations about my own death.

Finally, I began feeling better, and to feel even better, we upped the dose. However, the resulting chest pain became as constant as my irritability. Sherry begged for a change again. My mood was more than she could take, so I dropped back to the helpful dose and remained there.

With the new year, Sherry and I resolved to build a community of friendships. I made a date with a couple from our small group, though it was canceled twice due to snow and once due to sickness. I then made another date with a different couple, which was canceled twice due to sickness. In my effort to live in community, I was striking out. It seemed like most couples only had time for each other and their immediate family.

Still, I persisted. Eventually, we had some success. Those rare moments of community proved that Sherry and I desperately needed to get out more and socialize. We were floundering in isolation.

Chapter 27

Catching COVID and Perhaps Clarity

A Blessed Mess

When I face the mess
Corruption and politics
Deceit, greed, and oppression
On the outside, unable to look in
Locked inside, unable to escape
Too young to quit, too old to press on
Only God can make a way
Through the mess of this day
The days run together
Nothing seems to change
Burdens pile atop each other
Crushing my spirit, depressing me
Why is life like this?
What should I do?
I have no clue to the what or the why

I must adapt
I must overcome
I cannot do it alone,
God enlighten me
Encourage me
Today, everyday
Until this mess
Becomes a blessing

THE YEAR 2020 introduced the whole world to the coronavirus pandemic. I found myself stuck at home thanks to social distancing, with no elective cases and few clinic visits. It was the most eye-opening struggle in my life. Most of my past struggles had brought only darkness, depression, uncertainty, and discontent. However, the COVID-19 pandemic shed a bright light on my life.

That clarity did not come early in the pandemic.

At first, like so many people, I drank too much initially but repented after about a month. My adult kids, Sherry, and I were cloistered together and getting on each other's nerves. Ultimately, though, we decided to use this time of isolation to become closer as a family.

I realized what a fool I'd been. I had it so good. God called me to help heal others, and if that meant working on the medical floor like an intern, I was willing to try. I even started refreshing my memory by reading about the medical care of patients on ventilators. If it meant getting COVID-19 and being on a vent and dying, well, you can imagine how little that bothered me. Thank God it never got so bad at our hospital that I had to try to be a "real" doctor again. God made me a glorified carpenter, not an internist.

So I went back to work at the orthopaedic clinic. By God's grace, I never had to set foot on the hospital's medical floor. If I could just get through the pandemic, I was ready to operate again. I would finally, fully embrace being a surgeon.

I loved the people I worked with during the pandemic. We were making a huge difference in people's lives. I could see it in the eyes of a scared ninety-year-old with a masked face and gloved hands, as I removed her arm cast. She sat in her car because she was too afraid to come into the clinic. So I attached a long extension cord to the cast saw, took it outside, and knelt on the curb to perform the procedure. I also saw it on the face of a dementia patient when I visited him in the nursing home to assess his post-op knee wound. I saw it in the faces of my last post-op patients on telehealth appointments. Life had changed for all of us, but at least my meds were working. I was beginning to accept that my life was just the way God intended it.

When it was safe enough to return to my surgical practice, I relished every human contact. It was like having my sight restored. The appreciation I felt for my partners, staff, and patients was at an all-time high. It was great to be back doing what I was made to do—operate.

The only problem is that it was hurting me. The pain in my left elbow and wrist worsened until I had to stop working yet again in June 2020 to have another left elbow ulnar nerve release, medial epicondylectomy, left wrist Guyon's canal release, and pisiform bone excision. That meant six more weeks out of work with an immobilized elbow and wrist.

Thankfully, the surgery seemed to work out this time. All the pain and problems in the left elbow and wrist were gone.

To celebrate, Sherry and I went to Cape Coral, Florida, for a "pretend to be retired" trip. As one of the sunniest cities in the United States, Cape Coral's waterways flowed with serenity. We relaxed at the beach, picked up shells on Sanibel Island, and enjoyed some terrific seafood. We were ready to return to Cape Coral the day we left, but sadly, we never did.

Chapter 28

CLARITY

Salvation's Joy

Grace in the face
Of love and forgiveness
Illuminates my heart
With joy in your presence

For I gazed upon the face of God
And felt the warmth of His embrace
When I humbled myself to You
Who offered pardon and grace

My soul called out for You
And in love You came
Now my spirit leaps
At the very mention of Your name

I long for Your love
I thirst for Your affection
I have Your approval
I crave Your attention

Nothing comes between us
No bondage of guilt restrains
Now, finally, I rest in Your love
No shackles of fear to constrain

IN SEPTEMBER 2021, I had the delta variant of COVID-19. I was actually suffering from my second bout of COVID, even though I'd been fully vaccinated. After about eight days in quarantine, I was feeling a little better, so I decided to do something productive—take up writing again.

My first bout of COVID came from the alpha strain in December 2020, two days after I had a two-level cervical disk replacement surgery to control my severe neck and shoulder pain, along with my cervicogenic headaches. Work was taking a massive toll on my body, the pain causing me to lose sleep just as my wrist and elbow pain had done earlier in the year. Like all my other surgeries, the goal was to get my body fixed so I could get back to operating. It had become a way of life, getting operated on so I could operate on others.

Thankfully, the neck surgery went great, and recovery started so easily! Two days later, however, I slept for thirty-six hours straight. Then I slept about sixteen to eighteen hours a day for a week after that. I had COVID tests, but they were all negative. Sherry, who had been vaccinated, was suffering from anosmia (losing her sense of taste), but she tested negative as well. It was baffling. We knew we had received false negatives because all three of our vaccinated kids tested positive.

The pandemic took so much away from everyone. I am still haunted by it to this day. Chiefly, I think about all of the lives that were lost, but I also remember the profound sense of isolation. In-person classes were eliminated, forcing all the students and teachers to navigate the then-uncertain waters of Zoom. There was no live music, no in-seat dining at restaurants, and no in-person church worship.

My routine consisted of putting on a mask, going to work, then going home, stripping down in the utility room to do laundry, and finally showering off the germs. That was it. Occasionally, I might stop by the grocery store, but grocery stores had limits on how many customers could enter. Store aisles also forced customers to walk in one direction so they wouldn't pass by each other. Before putting away the groceries, I'd wipe them all down with a anti-viral wipe. It was a crazy way to live, as many of you no doubt remember.

Even so, Sherry and I kept our plans to drive to Gulf Shores during the Christmas and New Year season of 2020–2021. It was the second week of my first COVID infection, and I was still pretty sick. I slept through most of that vacation.

Carpe Diem

The year 2021 was supposed to be a new start for the world, and especially for me. My neck and shoulder pain were gone. I was doing better at moderating my alcohol intake. My reduced surgical case load was manageable, and I had no regrets over making less money. Without so much pain, my mood had improved.

I remained in the seminary cohort, at least initially, auditing a class on missions. However, the professor's ratio of the use of "I" to "Jesus" was about a hundred to one. His arrogance repelled me, and I began to wonder why I was wasting my time in the class. I was seeking community. I was also trying to find a way to become more relevant to the church, to God, to myself. I wanted to belong to something bigger than myself, but what I wanted most of all was to know God truly. While my time in the cohort had been valuable, it was clearly time to move on. Miles was right. The answers I was searching for were not going to be found by holing up in my office and studying with no clear purpose. So I quit. Again.

The summer of 2021 brought a more virulent and contagious delta variant of COVID, which extended the suffering of the global pandemic. Hospitals were overwhelmed again, mostly with unvaccinated people. Ironically, when President Trump was still in office during the pandemic, Democrats said they would never trust a vaccine that came out under his administration.[2] Then Senator Biden became president, and the script flipped. Now, Republicans became suspicious of the vaccine, and Democrats wholeheartedly embraced it. It made no sense.

Our nation was polarized, and the pandemic was made worse by our division. The people who suffered most were the ones waiting in emergency rooms for hours and even days, waiting for a hospital ICU bed to open up. Hospital overcrowding actually prevented me from being able to treat my own postoperative patient one time because my hospital was on diversion. The human right to access medical care was in jeopardy.

Stress levels were historically high, but I found relief by shutting off all social media and news. For a political junkie like me, that was hard. After two months of fasting from the news, I found clarity. The twenty-four-hour news networks and social media

---

2   Lauren Fox and Clare Foran, "Democrats Say They Need to Hear from Scientists, not Trump, That Vaccine Is Safe," CNN, September 15, 2020, https://www. cnn.com/2020/09/15/politics/democratic-reaction-covid-vaccine.

are ultimately just echo chambers that radicalize our thoughts. The more we listen, the angrier we feel. Yet we continue to listen. The whole system is designed to make us take in advertisements. I felt freer once I no longer had the burden of trying to figure it all out, without having to know who the "true enemy" was, if there was one.

Free from all that worry, my family and I set out to celebrate the summer. Spencer and Alex were graduating from graduate school. We had four big birthdays to celebrate. Sherry and I were turning fifty, Paige twenty-one, and Spencer twenty-five. We lived large, ate and drank, and were merry. All of this, along with surviving the pandemic, was only possible because of the excellent psychiatric care of Dr. Peri, to whom I will always be grateful.

Sherry and I planned a trip to the Grand Tetons to celebrate both of our birthdays at the beginning of July. Before we left, my neck pain returned, accompanied by a severe headache. I was devastated. The psychiatrist upped my Zoloft to one hundred milligrams, which did wonders to keep me from spiraling down the drain emotionally. I got a cervical epidural steroid injection the day before our trip. It did nothing.

During the trip, I gave myself intramuscular shots of Toradol and eventually Depomedrol. Trying to knock out the inflammation didn't work, so I started on Horizant, which gave some reprieve. But I knew I wouldn't be able to continue Horizant after the vacation because it affected my cognition. Despite the challenge, we had a great trip filled with a rodeo, a chuckwagon dinner show, an outdoor concert, hiking, floating, shopping, and dining out. We were doing all the things that the pandemic had taken away. Even with my neck pain, it was nice to see the world opening up again.

Sadly, the pain was in full force when I returned to work. I tried too many shots and pills to mention before finally starting physical therapy. One month of physical therapy seemed to be having some success, but then I became infected with the delta variant. It wrecked me. The day after my diagnosis, I got the monoclonal antibody infusion, which helped keep the case mild. Five solid days of rest alleviated my neck and headache pain. However, as soon as I began to feel better, I started working from home, and the neck pain and headache returned almost immediately. Imagine that. As it turns out, constantly craning my neck forward, staring at a screen, and forgetting proper posture results in pain.

And So It Ends

During my brief quarantine, I listened to the book *Knowing God* by J. I. Packer. I believe I found within those pages what I had always been looking for: how to know God. Packer takes readers on a journey through Scripture to show the beautiful character, attributes, and nature of God, leading to a deep desire to worship and to have a personal relationship with Father God. After listening to *Knowing God*, I was done trying to comprehend Him. I was done searching for the answers about my calling and what I'm supposed to be doing. I was done seeking solutions to all of my pain, or how to escape my mood disorder. I was done overanalyzing my drinking. I just needed to drink less. I was ready to be content and abide in His presence.

Finally, I could accept that I have my thorns in the flesh and in my mind. I could bear them without my mind constantly racing by leaning on God's sufficient grace and faithfully taking my medication.

In fact, when I first wrote this chapter back in 2021, this is how I concluded (and it's still true today):

I am blessed beyond measure. My marriage is great. My kids have turned out amazingly well. I'm so proud of them and so proud of Sherry's work at Hockman's Interiors! Life is good! I must do as my mother and father often told me. I must choose to be happy. My chief aim will be to glorify God and enjoy Him forever. One day, I will rise in a perfect resurrected body with a mind free from all sin and corruption, alive in a new heaven and new earth! Until then, I'll await my Savior's return with an open mind and open heart. See, turning fifty isn't so bad.

Turning fifty put me in a good headspace, so much so that I completed my memoirs on a high note. At the time, I was excited to end the book with hope. On the horizon were Paige's college graduation, Spencer's start of a new career, and Alex's beginning of law school. As if that weren't enough, all three children were engaged to be married. Everything seemed to be falling into place. God's grace had poured down from heaven and showered me with many blessings, despite the continued curse of an uncooperative body and mind.

Now, as I finally finish revisions on this book, I am about to turn fifty-two, and my family has grown by three. I have gained two daughters and a son through marriage. The weddings were some of the best experiences of my life. Nothing compares with walking your little girl down the aisle to a man you've come to love as your own son. Not that I'm playing favorites. I love my new daughters, too.

Although the work of a parent is never truly finished, my role as a father has shifted from protector and provider to counselor and cheerleader. I am thrilled with the transition. Watching Spencer, Alex, and Paige thrive in marriage not only fills my wife and me with joy, but also has deepened our faith in God. Our heavenly Father lovingly answered our prayers for each one of our children that they would find a spouse who wholeheartedly loves and serves Jesus. Our love, joy, and peace have increased and will continue to overflow with each new grandbaby that we trust God to bring our way (hopefully again and again).

And it looks like I will have plenty of time to spend with them, as my body has continued to betray my calling, forcing me into an early medical retirement. Still, even as I write, I find the *D* word too hard to accept, too hard even to write. I'll try: D-I-S-A-B-I-L-. See, I can't do it.

Twenty years into practice, my cervicogenic headaches, neck pain, left upper extremity ulnar nerve paresthesias, and Raynaud's disease severely limited my practice. About a year ago (at the time of this writing), I was ready to throw in the towel until I met with a pastor from church. Before the meeting, I had experienced a series of coital headaches and had to get a CT angiogram of my head to make sure I didn't have a tumor or aneurysm. I made the appointment with the pastor because I wanted to talk about whether I had reached the end of my rope.

The pastor had a recommendation he admitted was strange. After he reinforced my calling as a surgeon and reminded me of the great need in our country for medical personnel, he advised me to begin practicing guided Christian meditation daily. He offered his own podcast as a resource. Though he admitted it sounded a bit self-serving, he went on to explain how beneficial it had been for his chronic pain. So I tried it, and I've continued to do it nearly every day since. I highly recommend it. My anxiety and headaches greatly improved, and I continued my reduced surgical case load with less pain.

Alongside my daily meditation practice, I also began working out with a personal trainer, Tyson Oak, to build functional strength. Tyson has built my body back into the best shape it has been in since high school. He knows my limitations and pain, and he trains my body in such a way that I have increased my strength without harming myself. Getting a personal trainer has been a huge blessing, helping me accomplish what I could never have done on my own. He's a pretty good counselor, too.

With a stronger mind and body, I thought my career would last five or ten more years. Unfortunately, the L4/5 disk herniation I first experienced in 2018 has resulted in severe arthritis, which eventually began causing increased back pain and lower extremity paresthesias, despite an epidural injection, facet joint injections, a one-week steroid taper, home exercises, intramuscular Toradol injections, Advil (until my reflux forced me to quit taking it), Tylenol, and Horizant. Sadly, nothing helps. All I can do is hope it passes soon, but ultimately, it is time for my career as a surgeon to end. The occupational medicine doctor told me what I've told many of my own patients over the years: "Your career is destroying your body, and you need to find a new one."

As I write this, I am still grieving the loss of my calling. I'm sure readers can see the first four stages of grief throughout this book: denial, anger, bargaining, and depression. Hopefully, the mandate from my occupational medicine doctor will eventually bring me to the last stage—acceptance. But I'm not quite there yet. I have cried over the loss of my calling until I have no tears left. My life as a surgeon is over. Unbelievable!

Well, maybe the next phase will be better.

That seems hard to believe right now, especially since I have been diagnosed with psoriatic arthritis, and I'm staring down the possibility of a third left ulnar nerve surgery! The crippling hand and foot pain of my autoimmune inflammatory arthritis sounded the death knell for my ability to operate. I was forced to end my orthopaedic practice. But God is greater than all of these things, and I am committed to following His lead, knowing, finally truly *knowing* Him and that He is truly good!

Epilogue

ON MARCH 31, 2023, I performed my last total knee replacement and went home without any fanfare. Two months later, I saw my last patient in the clinic and again went home without any celebration. It was a bittersweet, yet necessary, ending. Three years later, I look back on those two days with a sense of relief. The weight of the responsibility a surgeon carries is only tolerated because he has no idea how heavy it is until he lays it down. Honestly, I am happy the sovereignty of God intervened and forced me to lay it down. The final stage of grief has passed.

Today, I still have the burden of living with chronic pain, but I am told by family and friends that I do it joyfully. Perhaps that is because I perceive God's purpose in it, which is to draw me closer to Him, teaching me to trust Him for each day's sufficient measure of grace, leading me to rely on His strength from moment to moment, and sustaining me with the ultimate hope of a resurrected glorified body, living forever face-to-face with the Father, Son, and Holy Spirit in a new heaven and earth where there will be no more pain and suffering.

Perhaps it is because I take better care of my mental and physical health. I did have a second revision of my left ulnar nerve surgery, and it was helpful. Hopefully, that will be my last surgery. My psychiatrist takes great care of my depression and anxiety, which I have accepted as simply part of how God made me.

I have a psychologist who offers wisdom, grace, and encouragement in the heavier moments of life. Friendships have taken on a much more meaningful role in life, which has influenced me to be alcohol free for nearly a year. A functional medicine doctor has helped me to have better health habits. Physical therapy and Pilates have been quite helpful for my neck and low back arthritis. All this care would likely not have been possible without my rheumatologist, who diligently worked with me to find a biologic treatment that has offered much-needed, though not complete, relief from the psoriatic arthritis.

I still follow my calling to serve. Despite all my complaining, serving as a surgeon did give me joy. I now serve as a men's group leader at church, an occasional Bible teacher for the fifty-plus group, and as a mentor to a couple of younger men. By God's grace, my life's experiences have made me who I am and who I am becoming. I have found that fostering transparent, vulnerable relationships with and among men lifts us all together to be more like Jesus. I also enjoy continuing to serve as a board member of Coyote Hill Foster Care Ministries. All proceeds from sales of this book will go straight to them.

Although the fatigue from my autoimmune disorder can determine my day's activities, I do my best not to let fatigue or pain determine my attitude. I think gratitude, especially for my family, plays a huge role in that. Sherry loves me fiercely, and I love her. Spencer, Alex, and Paige all got married within a year of each other. Each couple has given us a granddaughter, all three born within seven months of each other in 2025! I am most grateful that each granddaughter is growing up in a home that honors Jesus and freely accepts His grace. Each new little family is trying, as Sherry and I have done, to live *Soli Deo Gloria!*

I welcome thoughtful messages related to this book, as well as speaking and event inquiries, at contact@surgeonunmasked.com.

While I can't respond to every message, I will read them with care. Please note that I will not engage in unconstructive or adversarial dialogue.

If you or someone you know is in emotional distress or considering self-harm, help is available. Please call or text the 988 Suicide & Crisis Lifeline at 988 or visit 988lifeline.org. These services are free, confidential, and available 24/7. For urgent personal or pastoral needs, please seek support from trusted local professionals or clergy.

About the Author

David E. Hockman, MD, is a native of Missouri, where he stayed to build a career and a beautiful family. His special interest in helping people from a young age led him to his calling in medicine.

Dr. Hockman completed his undergraduate studies and medical school at the University of Missouri in Columbia. He then moved to Kansas for his orthopaedic surgery residency at the University of Kansas in Wichita, followed by a fellowship at the Anderson Orthopaedic Clinic and Research Institute in Alexandria, Virginia. There, he focused on adult reconstructive surgery.

In 2003, the Columbia Orthopaedic Group recruited Dr. Hockman to continue "Moving You Forward" in hip and knee replacement surgery. Since that time, he has performed over 7,500 joint replacements and has helped even more patients with nonoperative care. Dr. Hockman's goal as a surgeon was to glorify God by working to restore patient mobility and quality of life. He retired in 2023.

Today, he and his wife, Sherry, are members of the Crossing Church and have three adult children and three beautiful granddaughters. David currently serves on the board of trustees for Coyote Hill Foster Care Ministries and on the Crossing Men's Ministry leadership team. Sherry was a stay-at-home mom for fifteen years and now owns and operates Hockman Interiors at the Parkade Plaza.